GARETH EDWARDS
ON FISHING

Gareth Edwards on Fishing

GARETH EDWARDS
with
TONY PAWSON

COLLINS
8 Grafton Street, London W1
1984

William Collins Sons and Co Ltd
London · Glasgow · Sydney · Auckland
Toronto · Johannesburg

British Library Cataloguing in Publication Data

Edwards, Gareth
Gareth Edwards on fishing.
1. Fishing
I. Title II. Pawson, Tony
799.1'2'0924   SH439

ISBN 0 00 217051 5

Photoset in Linotron Sabon by
Rowland Phototypesetting Ltd
Bury St Edmunds, Suffolk

Made and printed in Great Britain by
William Collins Sons & Co. Ltd, Glasgow

CONTENTS

ILLUSTRATIONS

ACKNOWLEDGEMENT

My grateful thanks to Hardy Brothers of
Alnwick for generously allowing me to use
their tackle, and for many happy days on their
water.

1

Beyond the Black Mountain

'How does any one so active have the patience to fish?' That was a fair question of a boy who never seemed to stop running, except when crouching motionless as his worm came trotting back towards him down the little streams, or his small spinner brought the trout from their hiding places. But no one asked it who had seen me race down to the water, hurdling a wall as I went. No angler ever asked it, for they all knew how compelling is the attraction of a sport which has had just as much importance in my life as rugby.

Bryn Evans, the schoolmaster who helped develop my passionate interest, had at least some sympathy with such questioners. 'Be patient,' he would say as I urged him to drive faster over the Black Mountain. 'The fish will wait for us.' Or again: 'You're an athletic fisherman, Gareth. You push on ahead of me. You fish many more pools than I do. You catch more trout than I. But if you slowed down and fished as carefully and quietly as I, you would share more of the larger ones with me.'

In my thirties I can take my time and I do catch my share of large fish. But in youth I was as impatient to get to the water as any salmon is to leap upstream. In my village of Gwaun-cae-Gurwen the first road in which I lived was called Ger-y-afon – the road by the river. That was appropriate. So many roads in my life have led to rivers. But the little river in that mining village is not one to entice fishermen: when it's low the pools are so tiny you can't believe there are fish in them, and when it's high the coal dust seeps down to give the stream the name

'Yr Afon Ddu', the Black River. We caught some eels there and when at last I caught a small trout its mouth was black with coal dust and there was a ball of dust in its gullet. But it was still the most beautiful fish I'd ever seen. If you could love fishing there you could enjoy it anywhere; after the 'Afon Ddu' the pure, clear streams and the broad rivers were an endless delight.

From an early age there were two worlds for me, both full of excitement and interest, both totally different in character. There was community, school, and family life with its tasks, challenges and friendships. That centred round learning and sporting competition and was the stage on which I had to prove myself. There I was driven by an innate desire to excel, by the need to achieve and show myself ready to hold my own later in a larger world. As in most Welsh mining villages, for youngsters there was only one standard of excellence, one target at which to aim. To us anyone who played rugby for Cwmgors was a hero, for Swansea a superman, for Wales a god.

With all the boys in the village I packed into our main playground, Archie's Field, a narrow strip of wasteland belonging to a farmer who rarely bothered to chase us out and may have admired the precision with which we marked out the touchlines in sawdust. For me those communal games were as important as the internationals I imagined myself playing when on my own, or with my brothers. Soccer was important to me too and when I wasn't beating England by the odd last-minute try, I was scoring the winning goal for Manchester United against Arsenal. Whatever type of ball my father gave me it was soon worn out, or confiscated by neighbours like Mrs Davies if I kicked it too far into her garden.

On my own I could dream of being a Welsh rugby star; in the reality of those games in Archie's Field I knew I had speed, and athletic ability, and a feel for the game. And it was those talents that stopped me becoming a miner and took me to Millfield School to be given a wider education, wider contacts and an unrivalled training in sport. Striving for success as sprinter, hurdler, footballer while achieving good academic standards was a dedicated phase of my life. It was coloured, too, with excitement; the thrill of winning, the bitterness of failures were never to be more keenly felt. It was a demanding life into which I poured my youthful energy, my determination, my heart. The refreshment of spirit to sustain the success which brought me to Millfield came from another world on the other side of the Black Mountains.

The headmaster of the Primary School, Bryn Evans, was the man who took me over the great divide to the trout streams, the freedom, the peace of mind on the far slopes. Some five miles was all the distance between home and another world, another existence uncluttered by any anxious striving. I couldn't reach it quickly enough. When my brothers and I cycled there, our headlong descent down the winding road beyond the crest brought many a tumble; when my parents gave me a lift there, or Bryn Evans took me in his car, I willed them to go faster in my fever of impatience. When later I drove my own small Morris 1000 the remembered recklessness of my driving makes me shudder now, as I recall the two-wheel cornering.

So quickly were we out of the houses of the village and into open country. Our side of the mountains is bare and feature-less near the peak. Beyond was our fisherman's paradise. I can stop now at the summit and take in the lush beauty of the scene below, the wealth of trees in the valley, the gentle hills beyond, the cultivated fields, the red earth, the green foliage. Now I can wonder at the richness of trout waters there which were so freely available to us as boys: Sawdde River running close to the road for mile after mile, but hidden in its own deep gulleys. Absorbed in our fishing we were totally unaware of the few cars passing just yards above us, and remained unseen by their occupants. The Sawdde races down over its rocky bed as eager to reach the quiet of the valley as we were to hasten to its banks. It is all fast current, and little swirling pools, changing round every bend, mysterious and delightful. Other tributaries join as it broadens and slows lower down. These have the occasional deep run, a few larger trout, and more miles of water to explore in hope. And all that was ours to enjoy. Behind, if we looked back from the top of the Black Mountain, was a harsher landscape and along the distant coast was the shroud of smoke signalling the concentration of industry beyond the valley mines. That side of the divide eloquently symbolises a hard, ordered, working life; the other beckons to Elysian fields and a carefree existence beside running waters.

There was no philosophising and no stopping in those early days. My whole being was concentrated on reaching the stream in the shortest possible time to leave the longest possible time for fishing. There was just one point where I slowed momentarily on that headlong descent. There was a moment of destiny as my eyes searched the nameless little rivulet plunging down the slope to disappear under the road. It was our barometer brook: if it showed white anywhere on the hillside, if the colour of its water was a creamy brown, then we were sure to have trout in plenty; if it was a sad characterless trickle then we knew we would have to work hard for a basket of fish. On our side of the mountain the streams might be different in height and colour, but whatever was the state of the barometer brook, that was the state of the Sawdde and its related streams. There is a thrill in the first sight of a river which stays with you all your life. If the water is a light brown and the bottom clear to see in the shallows then there is an instant lift of the spirit: the fish will be feeding and moving and there is rich promise of good sport. Even now that will make me hurry to get the first cast in, though I can generally relax and take Bryn Evans's oft-repeated advice: 'Take your time. The fish will wait for you.' On those flying visits to the Sawdde I couldn't wait for the trout – especially when the barometer brook showed all set fair for good fishing.

The Sawdde trout are small and voracious. Six inches was the limit and we had several to put back below that small size. There were plenty of salmon parr too, with those distinctive thumbprint marks down their sides, and I was well briefed to return all of them. I might have hesitated regretfully over the larger ones, but back they all went. A half-pound trout was a good fish, a three-quarter pounder a monster. When my brother Gethin claimed to have been broken by a great fish – the spread hands indicated one of over two pounds – we didn't believe him. 'No, honest,' he kept repeating, close to tears. 'It *was* that big. I *saw* it. And it was so strong it broke the line.' Finally we went at his insistence to look where he claimed he had hooked it. He had indeed. For there it still lay, the line trailing behind. It was a sea-trout which had pushed into the upper reaches, and weighed perhaps three pounds or so: a huge fish which had given him the greatest thrill and the bitterest disappointment of his young life, though it was some consolation for Gethin that *we* shared the knowledge that he *had* hooked it at least.

My father would have preferred me to spend my time becoming a musician, but he readily accepted my lack of interest in the cornet and supported me in my fishing as in my rugby. In neither was he knowledgeable enough to give much help, and the fishing equipment he gave me was a comic mixture. To search out the Sawdde I had a small trout fly rod, but a spinning reel. I had to invent my own method of using them. My favoured lure was a size O Mepps, which I flicked up a few yards into each little pool. There was no time to wind in, so I recovered a yard or two by hand after each cast. When a trout took, my strike was violent – so often you could *see* them take in that clear water – and the small ones would fly over my head into the bracken. We travelled light, unburdened with complex equipment or theories, covering miles of the river and taking a dozen trout or so, depending on the state of the water. We never stopped to wonder how there could be such an apparently limitless supply in so small a stream, whose pools never appeared to contain a living creature when first you peered into them. We concentrated on one thing, and one thing only – catching as many trout as we could.

When I had progressed to wearing waders I often had to earn my fish the hard way. My parents would drop me by the river and tell me to hitch-hike home at the end of the day, but cars were few and mostly filled with families of tourists, with no spare room for a dripping youth with his rod and trout. So it was the long walk back after a tiring day. Only when you stopped fishing did you notice you *were* tired: then the hard climb up the mountain and the weary walk home was a depressing enough prospect, especially when there were few trout in the bag. And those waders would chafe the shins, giving you 'welly rub' as we called it – and very sore it was. Fishing may not be as physical as rugby, but it did have its little hazards and injuries – sore shins, grazes from falling off cycles, and cuts from slithering over rocks!

In hindsight it was good to start with makeshift equipment. It meant I had to be inventive and adaptable. It also forced me to learn absolute control of the rod and understand its capabilities. In effect I was also learning two techniques at once, for the Mepps spinner was little bigger than a trout fly and my fishing was more akin to upstream flyfishing than to spinning.

The first accessory I acquired remains to me the most important adjunct of such fishing. It was a wicker basket; whenever I go after trout I always carry one. There was a ritual about it which was an essential part of the day. I would cover the bottom with damp ferns and lay the fish on them with loving care. The plump half-pounders with red spots and bright yellow bellies highlighted against the green of the ferns made the most satisfying picture imaginable. And soon my fishing tackle too had been taken in hand. In school Bryn Evans was a meticulous and forbidding character (with the aura of respect he generated I still find it hard not to write *Mr* Bryn Evans). But once he appreciated my love of fishing he became the organiser of fishing expeditions, an entertaining companion on whose words I hung, and the kindest of mentors. He laughed at my antics when first he watched me and promptly arranged for me to have matching equipment. Once I was complete with spinning rod he took me further afield and taught me how to catch more and bigger fish. Where the Sawdde reached the valley another stream meandered down to join it. Its lower reaches flowed through a farm and the owner, like so many Welsh farmers, was generous enough to let us fish along its banks. There my appetite was whetted by watching Bryn catch a trout of around two pounds, enticed out from its lie under a steep bank. I dreamed of doing the same myself, but my hurried fishing was better suited to catching smaller trout. There were plenty of those and I usually caught at least as many as Bryn. On the way back we always stopped on the home slopes of the Black Mountain, laid out the bag, and admired the varied colouring and shapes of the fish. Then we would divide up the catch and as often as not I had a dozen to take home with me. How proud I was to show them off and take some round to friends or relatives.

Part of fishing's appeal to me is in its being a lonely and self-contained sport. You are absorbed in the music of the waters, the beauty of the environment, the river's changing character, and the search for taking fish. Other humans can be intrusive, limiting the freedom, disturbing the peace, restricting the scope. Perhaps that's why the river fishing with which I started has always attracted me so much more than the somewhat artificial fishing on stocked lakes and reservoirs. These 'put and take' waters serve a purpose and greatly increase the numbers who can enjoy the sport, but such well organised fisheries, with their armadas of boats or crowded banks, don't excite me as much as rivers. In the fast streams, too, the fish have added power as they fight you with the current to aid them, and for me there is more skill in the locating and stalking of fish in streams. That surely is angling's chief attraction; it is a lonely battle of wits. Yet fishing is also a companionable sport and for full enjoyment experiences have to be shared. That means fishing with someone with whom you are quite relaxed and who shares the same passion for the sport, or being able to talk over the day at its end with like-minded anglers. How fortunate I was to have brothers who enjoyed fishing and the likes of Bryn Evans to stimulate and share my enthusiasm. Bryn was born with a passion for fishing. Anyone can make himself into a competent angler by taking trouble: if he reads the textbooks and takes lessons he will soon be able to cast well and catch fish. But there is much more to fishing than the mechanics and tackle. The famous G. E. M. Skues in his essays has 'Mr Castwell' as a figure of fun, not as a paragon. To be really effective, to get full value from the sport, you must be born with it in your veins. Over three hundred years ago Izaak Walton, the father of anglers, expressed that exactly: 'The question is whether you be capable of learning it? For angling is somewhat like poetry, men are to be born so: I mean with inclinations to it, though both may be heightened by discourse and practice: but he that hopes to be a good angler, must not only bring an enquiring, searching, observing wit, but he must bring a measure of hope and patience, and a love of and propensity to the art itself.'

No wonder *The Compleat Angler* hasn't lost its attraction, has already run to over four hundred editions or re-issues, and has claim to be the most popular book after the Bible. There are dull passages of philosophy in it and out-dated angling advice, but old Izaak understood fishermen's minds, had a feel for the countryside, and some eternal truths to pass on. He knew what mattered all right! As he wrote: 'For I tell you, Scholar, fishing is an art, or at least it is an art to catch fish.' Catching fish is indeed the yardstick and the lucky ones are born with an instinct for it, like a splendid local character with whom I loved to fish, Hywel Awful. Their tackle may be a disgrace, their fly-tying a joke, their casting questionable. Yet their instinct for catching fish is superior to the well-equipped, well-taught angler who can't match their basket and is therefore less master of the art for all his outward show of excellence. Happily I have always had some of that instinct, and happily I was launched on what Izaak clearly regarded as the pinnacle of fishing – trout fishing. 'Is it not an art to deceive a Trout! A Trout that is more sharp-sighted than any hawk and more watchful and timorous than your high-mettled Merlin is bold?' Now that I could deceive so many on the Sawdde I had the confidence and capability for bigger game.

Having been born with that love of fishing, each day over the Black Mountain was precious to me whether we ended with three or thirty. How hard it is for those who are not natural fishermen to appreciate the vital part it plays in our lives. That great Welshman, David Lloyd George, was perceptive about so many things but this he could not understand: of the man who was Foreign Secretary at the outbreak of the First World War he wrote with asperity and total bewilderment: 'Lord Grey might be anything he likes in public life, yet he prefers to waste his time fishing.' But for me and most of us fishermen Lord Grey had his priorities right. His summary of a very full life must touch a chord with all of us: 'When an angler reviews the pleasures of life he will be glad he has been an angler. For he will look back on days radiant with happiness, peaks and peaks of pleasure.' There were plenty of days radiant with happiness as I fished the Sawdde in boyhood, but the true peaks of pleasure were still to come. Again, it was Bryn Evans who pointed the way. 'We are going *draw'r wlad*' he told me as he picked me up one day. The drive was longer than usual and I was more impatient than usual, wondering where *was* 'out to the country' and what might be at the end of the mystery tour. At last we stopped and walked down to a bridge. As we gazed over I caught my breath. This was indeed the end of the rainbow, the river of my dreams.

2

Trout *Draw'r Wlad*

Draw'r wlad came to mean for me a trip to the top reaches of the Cothi River beyond Pumsaint. Mention the Cothi in Wales and most anglers associate it with large sea-trout. There are indeed great runs of these in the Towy, with sizeable shoals diverting up to the Cothi to give some marvellous night sea-trout fishing in its lower reaches. Above Pumsaint the sea-trout are few, but the brown trout are numerous and of much better average size than I had encountered down on the Sawdde.

It is an enchanted setting in which to catch fish. The river is clear and easy to cover as it glides or bustles through the valley, but there is plenty of vegetation on the banks and many holding places where tree roots jut into the water or branches overhang the stream. There are fast runs, but some deep, still places as well. Each pool is different from the last, each holding the promise of trout, and each with some new challenge for the angler – a difficult cast, tree branches to work under, the main lies hard to determine; always something to stimulate interest and test skill. The level floor of the valley has space for the river to wind and wander after rushing down from its source in the mountains, but the valley itself is isolated, and shut in by steep wooded slopes on either side. You are lost from the world as you follow the river through that quiet and lovely setting.

The valley stirred my imagination, but it was the river which made my pulse beat faster: you only had to look at it to know there were lots of trout there. As often as not you could see them take the little Mepps, with a sudden flash of yellow in the bright water. They were beautiful plump fish with vivid red spots; fifteen or twenty in a day made an imposing basket. Before long I knew the water intimately and with experience began to know with certainty the chief lies. That added spice to the fishing. When the water was clear you could so easily frighten the fish with a bad cast: you had to get it right first time if you wanted to take a fish in each little pool. That meant being absolutely precise with the first cast and ensuring no great splash as the Mepps entered the water; then you needed to keep the spinner moving fast from the moment it hit the surface. The difference between getting it right and a sloppy first cast might be a couple of trout in the day rather than twenty. That taught you fast!

It was a splendid place too for learning the way fish change position in different heights of water. When it is low the few you catch are in the runs and you look for turbulence as a target for your spinner. When it's in spate and muddy you take trout in the little eddies and at the side of the main currents. When it was fining down after rain, with that exciting light brown look, you expected fish everywhere. Only once was I disappointed when it had that colour. It was the first day of the season when I went with Hywel Awful to where the Bran joins the Cothi. When we saw the state of the water I told him we would make a killing that day. We caught nothing. What I hadn't realised was that when the water is really cold, as it was that March day, the fish will stay down and be reluctant to feed whatever the colour and height. You can read about it in books, but there's no substitute for a practical experience like that to fix it in the mind! And there were few lessons about spinning for trout in small clear streams that the Cothi couldn't teach me.

There were other lessons for me back at Gwaun-cae-Gurwen when our village started a fishing club. The first surprise was how many keen and knowledgeable anglers there were in the village, whom I had never suspected of being fishermen, let alone expert ones. It is a solitary sport and many prefer to keep themselves to themselves when out on the rivers, but most anglers seem ready enough to share their knowledge if prompted, and there were many such in our village. Evans the Minister had already helped me, realising that I was more at ease on the river bank than in Chapel. Now there were others to teach fly-tying, to show slides and films, to give talks on practical aspects of fishing.

We only made small individual contributions to the club, but helped in raising funds by the usual variety of methods. Leading businessmen in the village also assisted with donations and guaranteed bank loans as the venture grew into a major communal effort. As a result the club was able to acquire several interesting stretches of water on which many of us younger ones were able to extend our fishing range. There were beats of one and a half miles on Towy and Usk to enjoy and a mile or so on the Taff and the Cothi. Now Bryn Evans had a wider range of suggestions for our outings. 'What do you want? Catching trout is it? Or a try for a salmon? Or a sea-trout on the Cothi?' Going trouting was still my first choice, my first love.

That side of fishing was the most important aspect for me, but I enjoyed also the meetings in the Buffalo Club – the Buffs as we called it – and the fly-tying lessons in the local school. As always when fishermen get together there was much to learn, many ideas to evaluate. The talks by a biologist were of particular interest to me – they helped me to understand more about game fish, their habits and their feeding patterns. That's all basic essential knowledge if you want to be a competent angler. Still, theory then had only a limited attraction for me. My feeling about these sessions at Buffs or the school was that I most enjoyed tying flies with the rest and learning from each other. We would laugh at our mistakes and swap stories as we tied. Such lessons also taught me something about fly patterns and which to use. There was a peculiar satisfaction when I caught a trout on a fly I'd tied myself but it wasn't a skill I found I had any particular interest in or ability to practise on my own. Being able to tie them yourself is a different craft which can be fascinating in itself but which doesn't necessarily catch you any more fish. So I absorbed something from the lessons, but my real learning was still in the growing store of experience from my own hunting and catching trout, my own observation of how they reacted. For me the importance of the club was in the new fishing friends it brought, the appreciation of how important fishing was in the lives of so many people, and in having my appetite further whetted by the stories of great fish or great catches.

One of the main influences on my fishing development was a man I had already met outside the club. Hywel Awful was a unique character, difficult to know well and just as difficult to describe. His name itself gives a good impression of the general opinion of him. He was known as the hard man of Gwaun-cae-Gurwen. What the Canterbury team in New Zealand once did to us on a Lions tour was as nothing to the terrible things Hywel was said to have done on the rugby field. And when he was credited with responsibility for breaking a leg, inevitably it was the *referee's* leg. It was a great sadness for me later when I heard that he had been arrested for poaching and had compounded the offence by punching the water bailiff. That was no surprise to the village, who regarded him as a kind of Andy Capp character – awful but slightly smaller than life. But for me he was witty, kind, unafraid, full of interesting ideas – and nonchalant. It was that nonchalance, which was largely responsible for his reputation: his throwaway remarks were never taken seriously, though often they were wise and penetrating. And because he wasn't bothered what people thought about him they thought the worst. But even in the worst of his actions there was some wild logic, as with the poaching episode. He had poached for years. Everyone knew it, no one bothered, and he never tried to conceal it. So when someone arrested him for it he felt betrayed, victim of a madman's whim, and when not even his silver-tongued oratory made any impression he swung his fist to relieve his feelings. 'It was a stupid thing to do, Gar,' he confided to me when I chided him about it. 'It could only make a bad situation worse.' Then a broad smile lit his face. 'But it was a great satisfaction, wasn't it?'

Hywel loved poaching because of the excitement and the extra skill of mixing his famous pastes, which were deadly for trout. In fact he had no need of them, for he was an angler of remarkable ability who always caught more fish than others – legitimately. Because no one took him seriously they ascribed his great catches to poaching, or to luck, or to any other of the excuses less successful anglers dream up to explain the success of others. But I went out with him often and I knew better. He was careless about his tackle. His spinners were rusty. His rod was chucked in the coal shed after use and taken out again only when he next went fishing. His line was frayed, his flies tatty – but he had a wonderful instinct for fish. My eyes are very sharp, but in the river Hywel would see fish long before I could. And if he couldn't see them he sensed where they would be, what they would take, and had enough skill to put his lure where he wanted it. For me he was an amusing companion on fishing expeditions and there was much to be learnt by watching him: you can absorb a little of the special feel for catching fish if you watch them enough. Such fishing 'instinct' is the same kind of skill we attribute to 'green-fingered' gardeners. You can't define it, but it works. I thought of Hywel's 'green-fingered' fishing when I read what Moc Morgan, the enthusiastic secretary of the Welsh Salmon and Trout Association, wrote about one of the Welsh Internationals with whom he fished. 'Evan Owen was the most remarkable fly-fishing competitor it's been my privilege to meet. He was a collier, who lived only for his fishing. His tackle was a disgrace, fit only for the junk yard. Yet in Evan's hard, blue-stained hand that tackle regularly took fish when the rest of us were struggling. His flies and his theories were both absurd by normal angling standards. Yet he just went on catching fish when others failed. For many years Evan fished with distinction in the Welsh International team. He seemed devoid of all the qualities expected of an efficient angler – except the crucial one of catching fish. Evan's outstanding service to the national team was finally rewarded by appointment as captain. For him that was an honour valued above all else, a life's ambition achieved.'

Hywel Awful and Evan Owen were clearly similar types of fishermen, though differently motivated. You should always judge anglers by the fish they catch, not by their expensive equipment, or measured casting. And by that standard of judgement Hywel was a *very* good angler. His kindness was later evident, too, in never trying to involve me in his poaching activities. He understood how it would look in the papers if a Welsh rugby star were found poaching – even if he didn't punch the bailiff in the eye! He merely aimed to pass on his own talent for catching fish on spinner or fly. Others might see him as a crude or comic character. To me he was a good friend, an expert fisherman, and a man who helped refine that indefinable sixth sense of how to catch fish that every effective angler develops.

Hywel was certainly not alone in enjoying a bit of poaching, as can be confirmed by Haydn Jones, manager of the prestigious Grafham Water in succession to that fine Welsh fisherman, David Fleming Jones. Haydn was for long a Welsh Water Authority bailiff and has a fund of stories about what went on in taking fish out of the Towy, Teifi, and Cothi. Compared to the poaching he has seen, Hywel's salmon roe and special pastes almost qualified as fishing! Haydn recalls the days when it was said of the Cothi that none of the salmon and sea-trout which swum up it ever swum down again – they were all driven back in the boot of a car!

'I made a formidable collection of fish spears and gaffs for poaching, including a most ingenious home-made gaff with a jaw which closed to prevent any fish slipping off after being impaled. The curator of Cardiff Museum asked for the collection and that's where it went.

'I once caught a local parson poaching. On his way to the river he passed close to where I was concealed and I watched him at work with a light. As he was coming back carrying a salmon I called to him, "What have you got there, Reverend?" He was just getting over a stile and the shock was such that he fell off. Then he rushed back to the Manse, locking the door and refusing to let me in. And his language – I've never heard anything like it! But he was very smooth-spoken in court, claiming mistaken identity and getting off. A month later two of us caught him at it again. No chance of mistaken identity that time and he was fined £30.

'Early on I partnered a formidable bailiff. Isaac was a giant of a man over six foot and broad with it. He always carried a huge blackthorn cudgel and was so keen he frightened me on occasions! Once he stopped a car after a tip-off and asked the driver to open the boot. It was locked and the driver refused. "I'll count three then I'll open it if you won't," said Isaac. The count was the fastest I've heard and as it finished he crashed the cudgel down, nearly splitting the boot in two and making it fly open. I held by breath – Isaac and I would have to pay for the damage if there was nothing there. But seven salmon were in the remains of that boot.

'Isaac could look after himself well enough, but for a time he had a ferocious Alsatian with him. Once at night, hearing movement in the bushes, he slipped the dog. Murderous sounds ensued. As we raced towards the noise I shouted urgently, "He'll kill him!" So he had – but it was a sheep the dog had killed. That's the only time I saw Isaac in a panic, and I had to help him bury the carcass. The Alsatian didn't come out with him again.

'There were some entertaining characters among the poachers and in its way it was a friendly war we waged, before the organised gangs moved in. One night I caught one of my "regulars" red-handed as he killed a small salmon. "Don't be hard on me," he said, "my old father's at death's door, and the one thing he fancies is a taste of salmon. How could I refuse a dying parent's request? So I just took this small one, as you see." By then I'd seen four more fish hidden in the ferns. "What are you trying to do," I asked, "kill him off early from a surfeit of salmon?"

'The poachers' mecca was the Cenarth Falls on the Teifi where the river runs through a narrow gorge. On the rocks there you can see footholds worn down by generations of poachers. Below the falls there were always coracles bobbing about, and nets everywhere. You had to stand well back if you ordered a coracle out, or you might be chopped down at the knees with the blade of an oar. It was here I had a remarkable experience years ago. I was amazed to see a rod top sticking out of the water as it swirled round in an eddy near the bank. I managed to grasp it and against strong resistance recovered the rest of the rod. There was a hand clamped round the butt, and when I pulled on that a drowning man surfaced. He was an Italian prisoner-of-war who had fallen in when fishing, couldn't swim, and would never have survived had he not kept hold of that rod.'

Hywel and his wife ran the local fish and chip shop; it was a good social centre in the evenings. Hywel might not come back from the pub until nearly eleven at night and then we would yarn on, but often I was up again long before dawn, eager to be off fishing once more and catch that early morning time when trout are often feeding. If that involved being taken over the Black Mountain by Bryn Evans I would have to creep up below his bedroom window and throw stones to wake him. By the time the club acquired some water on the Usk I had my own small car for the drive beyond Brecon. We had joined together to rent the beat and it was well worth it. In its higher reaches, the Usk is still wider than the top of the Cothi and more varied to fish; it's mostly flyfishing only on this part of the Usk and that inevitably broadened my range, but in its character, its fast flow and its clear water the river was very similar to the Cothi. There were occasional great hatches of fly when the Usk would boil with rising trout but I never fished dry fly, finding they were then just as eager to take conventional wet fly patterns fished downstream; that was how I caught my trout. The greatest thrill, and one of the most productive methods, was dapping the dropper across the eddies beside a main current: often this brought a slashing take, with the trout springing half out of the water to seize the fly. Such rises called for moderation in the strike or you broke the fine cast. In all sport the main problem is to be both tense and relaxed: you need to be keyed up and concentrating, but if you are too taut you fumble your chances. Usk trout have to be quickly struck, and firmly tightened onto the hook. If you are dreamy you miss the rise; if you are too tense you react too hard to the sudden sight or feel of a fish, and smash the cast by the jerk of your rod.

Another influence on my early fishing was 'Ginger' Jones, a former champion boxer. The only thing he was punch-drunk over was catching trout or salmon. He kept a fishing tackle shop in Pontadawe and it was from him that I acquired my first trout flyfishing rod – my most treasured possession at the time. 'Ginger' taught me a lot about tackle and flies and was an expert guide on our many fishing expeditions together.

As I became more involved with Welsh rugby and success in sport brought more demands on my time, I had less and less opportunity to go trouting, though the love of it has never left me. Yet a new aspect of fishing began to absorb all my interest. Variety is one of angling's charms, and it's natural to start small then move on to bigger game. By the time I was leaving Millfield I was ready to go after sea-trout and salmon. I found the pursuit of them so fascinating it left me little inclination for anything else. When I have gone a month or so without catching a salmon I sympathise with the friend who said recently, 'Why don't I go back to trout fishing? I used to catch several every day. Now I go days without moving anything. Am I wasting my time on salmon?' He knew he wasn't, because with salmon the hunt is as important as the catching. But he had a point: the new love shouldn't entirely drive out the old. After all the pleasure it has given me in the past I can't give up river-fishing for trout. It just takes second place for the time being.

3

Bigger Game

Pound for pound sea-trout fight harder than any other river fish I've hooked, except perhaps the New Zealand rainbows in the streams round Taupo Lake. That makes them an exciting quarry at any time, but particularly at night when the reel seems to scream louder in the stillness, and the dark makes landing them that much harder. A six-pound sea-trout taken then can make all other fishing seem dull by comparison. In May and June the Towy and the Cothi have big runs of these splendid fish.

There are experiences in plenty to trigger memories when I can't get down to the river for this very special type of fishing. In the car I keep a tape which vividly conjures up the setting and sounds of such epic battles in dusk or dark. This is the Hugh Falkus tape on catching sea-trout; apart from much sensible advice it helps you picture a typical evening when the sport is at its best. It is warm and cloudy as the light fades. An owl hoots from the darkening trees, plainly heard above the gentle lap of running water from the low clear river. Soon comes the splash of a moving sea-trout, then more and more of them to quicken the pulses. Occasionally there is the unmistakable wallop of a heavy fish, as restless as the angler on the bank waiting for it to be dark enough to start without disturbing these scary fish. Listening to the description and the sounds of one such heavyweight being stalked and caught puts me in the right mood for a night on the Towy, with the confident expectation of turning into reality the scene so evocatively described by Hugh.

Falkus's long study has made him such an authority on all types of sea-trout fishing that it's not surprising I should find much of the advice he gives echoed in my own experience. This is a shy fish and it has to be hunted with stealth. If you want good catches you must always move quietly, avoid the skyline in the light, or flashing torches riverwards in the dark. It is a fish which shoals and you need to identify in daylight where the shoals are, unless you know this already from long association with one river.

Sea-trout are often active on the surface (and best fished for with floating line) from dusk to midnight. Thereafter they go quieter and deeper, and sunk line, or sink tip more usually on the Towy, is best. But as Falkus says, the lack of visible activity doesn't mean you won't go on catching from midnight to dawn – and even if there is less chance of large numbers in that period there is more chance of a really big fish. One point that I feel is over-emphasised, even by Hugh, is that of *not* starting until the light has faded completely. Certainly that is good advice as regards not disturbing the key place you are going to fish: beginning too early and frightening them in the lie may be the difference between a good bag and a blank, since sea-trout grow much more confident in the dark but are so easily put down in the twilight. But it is also true that the main taking time is from dusk to midnight and if you have plenty of water to fish you want to make the most of it. Don't hesitate to start as soon as the fish begin to move. Reserve the best place undisturbed for that special time between ten and midnight, but try the other pools from the moment the light begins to fade. If you are stealthy enough and cast softly enough you can often get plenty of fish. Indeed Ken Edwards, keeper of the Abercothi Water on the Towy, is one of the most successful sea-trout fishermen I know, and he catches nearly all his at dusk without bothering to wait for the dark.

Daylight reconnaissance also needs to do more than spot fish unless you know the river well. Hours before dark it pays to test the wading and the length of casting required in your chosen night spot. On the Towy the wading in some of the good pools can be difficult by day, with the spines of slippery-sided rock sliding away into deep gulleys or holes, but what is merely difficult by day becomes treacherous indeed by night when you cannot see the hazards or guess the depth of water a yard or two away. So you need to plot and memorise your route by day if you have to wade at night. You must measure exactly, too, the length of line to cast from your wading position to cover the main lies. That is important. Often you need to cast close to the far bank because the lies are there or because your fly needs to land there if it is to work properly across the narrow gutters which are the killing areas in some of our Towy pools. As the light fades so does the far bank until it looks more distant than it is: it's all too easy to overcast in the dark and lose your fly unless you have made exact measurement in advance.

Hugh Falkus's advice on flies is excellent, not least for the simplicity of having only five main patterns. How often we overload ourselves with too much equipment, too many flies, too many options to worry about! Even so, I have needed only two of his suggestions: the Medicine fly catches large numbers, and the tandem lure with peacock herl is also effective. The floating lure is of little use on my main beat on the Towy since many of the taking areas have too fast a current for any ripple they make to attract the fish. And for me the Falkus 'secret weapon', involving the use of maggots and a trailing treble, can remain on the secret list. Maggots are banned on the Welsh sea-trout rivers I fish – and I'm delighted at that. Maggots in the mass I can just accept, but individual squirming maggots give me the shivers! Handling them in the dark would destroy some of the pleasure of night fishing for me and add an unnecessary complication. Successful maggots may be in snaring sea-trout, but artificial flies are good enough for me.

In all other ways the Falkus tape has been an inspiration, and it was only by an odd chance that I acquired it. My interest in soccer has remained from boyhood days, and John Toshack is a great friend and golfing partner of mine. So when John was piloting Swansea to the First Division I went to watch the crucial match against Preston. To my surprise I found myself talking sea-trout at the interval with a man I'd never met before who said he would send me the tape. Such casual offers are rarely followed up, but a couple of days later there was a kindly letter from Hugh together with the tapes on sea-trout and salmon fishing his friend had asked him to send.

It was another such chance encounter which first sparked my real interest in sea-trout, and started one of my closest fishing friendships. I was in a Neath restaurant talking enthusiastically about some early experiences on the Teifi and becoming lyrical about having caught several up to two pounds. A man looked through the curtain separating us from the next table and broke in on the conversation to say, 'It's time you did some proper sea-trout fishing. We throw back shrimps like that. Come and fish the Towy and *then* you'll understand what the sport is about.' That was my first introduction to a Swansea solicitor, Graham Evans, and through him to the Towy and Cothi. What peaks of pleasure have stemmed from that chance meeting!

Night fishing for sea-trout requires such different techniques. I was fortunate to be shown the way by skilled anglers. You do need good advice or instruction before starting if you are to have any early success. Anne Voss Bark, who, like her husband Conrad, is such a noted angler, caters for this at the delightful Arundell Arms at Lifton in Devonshire. She has made the hotel into a premier fishing centre over the past twenty years; it has over twenty miles of water on the Tamar and tributaries. The best sea-trout fishing is in the Lydd, as the fish swim swiftly up the Tamar into its clearer, cleaner water. The run of sea-trout begins in June, with the week following a high tide a particularly productive time.

It became obvious that many of the guests who were good daytime fishermen caught few at night compared to those who were well versed in this type of fishing, so recently the fishery manager, Roy Buckingham, has organised a series of courses in night fishing. Roy is a former Welsh open casting champion and a qualified Association of Professional Game Angling

Instructor. He is assisted by another very experienced fisher-man, David Pilkington. Their teaching method proved so successful that the first course of six caught some forty sea-trout in their two nights on the river. What did Roy teach as the important aspects?

'It has been rightly said that the further south you go from Scotland the harder sea-trout are to catch. We have developed methods of taking a number here by day using small weighted flies – mainly size 10 Black and Peacock Spiders or the Coachman, which is so effective on West Country rivers for brown and sea-trout. We start the course by day partly to confirm that their daytime technique is adequate, but mainly to show them night methods when they can still see what they are doing.

'If you fish with only one fly, we advise starting with a small one and, if nothing happens, to quickly change up to the larger flies. Right size of fly often depends on the amount of light in the sky, but sea-trout are so unpredictable: some evenings a small size 10 fly will catch fish all night; at other times you have to change up to a big lure soon after dark. Myself, I use a team of three flies, large on the tail and two small flies on the droppers. I rarely change the droppers, but the tail fly is often changed for a 'skater' if things go quiet. The first thing you notice about beginners is how easily they lose their casting rhythm as well as their bearings in the unfamiliar dark. They cast well for half-an-hour or so then begin to flag, putting no effort into it. Then I stand behind them, hold the rod and do a few casts with a little more effort than usual to get the message over.

'On moonlight nights we advise using smaller flies un-weighted. Muddlers can be very effective, and late in the season Daddy Longlegs may attract a fish. A dry fly skating on the surface can also have considerable success. Instead of the cork Hugh Falkus suggests, we use a piece of Ethafoam with a hook in it and that works well!'

David Pilkington has fished these rivers for years after a boyhood start on the Hodder, the Lune and the moorland streams of Lancashire, which then were plentifully stocked with small trout. He has devised several of the flies which do well on the Arundell Arms water.

'The big lure flies for fishing late I've developed from patterns suggested by T. C. Kingsmill Moore in that sea-trout classic *A Man May Fish*. Blue or black are the best colours and I tie a palmered fly on size 4 long shank partridge hooks. The dry fly skating on the surface often brings them up, but is better fished with a dropper: it's usually the wake of the tail fly which attracts them, but then the dropper which they take. You can fish the same place down several times with two wet flies and get no offer. Then put on a large dry fly and skate it over the surface leaving the same dropper and you may get a number of takes. The large flies are usually well enough weighted by their heavy hook. If you want to weight a wet fly for daytime fishing a good tip is to use the foil off wine bottles if you don't have any copper wire. In any case you can fold the foil more neatly over the body of the fly and it will sink faster.

'Night sea-trout fishing is an art, and the basics need to be mastered early. The main problem for beginners – and five of our first course had never fished at night before – is in judging distance in the dark and in knowing how much line to have out so that you cover the water without getting caught in the far bank. I teach them to measure the distance they will be casting by pulling line from the reel with the same length of pull each time. By starting with the end of the fly line level with the rod butt, they will already have enough line out to cast 9 yards (assuming a 9 ft rod, and the same length of line, and leader to start). Each arm-length of line then pulled out is counted until the fly is landing just short of the far bank, and there is the maximum needed for that particular stance.

'If the individual's casting technique is good enough then it's best to use two flies at night. The dropper can be very effective, but it can also cause a number of tangles unless you are reasonably skilful. Dusk can be a very good time as the fish come on the move, and I advise fishing then in another pool, if one is available, saving your night spot until it is too dark to

A superb sea-trout stretch on the Towy at Llandovery.

Tony Pawson casts a floating line into Avington's middle lake.

I'm using a popular and effective fly for the Tweed, Gordon's Fancy, and checking that the line isn't frayed.

Below:
Wading near The Bushes on the Tweed — I think it's a nice change from being in the boat.

disturb the sea-trout and put them down. We fish floating lines right through the night. Early on the fish take better near the surface, and late on you should be using large flies which will be heavy enough to get well down even with a floater. Most of the sea-trout are going to be taken in shallow water between two and four feet, so there is no need for sinking lines – at least in our small rivers.

'The first course was scheduled to fish only from 9.00 pm to midnight on its first night on the river. They were so absorbed they were still there at five in the morning! Dusk to midnight is often the best time. But there are many nights when a lot of anglers go home at midnight with very little – and those of us who stay on do very well later.'

The enjoyment of sea-trout fishing at night is enhanced if you go with friends. On your own there can be eerie and lonely periods of the night if fishing is slack and the imagination lively. And where wading is treacherous in the dark it's good to have help handy should an accident occur. But primarily it adds to the pleasure to share others' excitement at catching these marvellously sporting fish, to be kept alert as they have takes while the river seems dead to you, to indulge in friendly rivalry, and to enliven the night with humour when the fishing is dull. On one such night I was out on the River Towy with Graham Evans, his brother John and another close friend, Norman Jenkins, or Jenks to his pals. There was no moon, the darkness was stifling, the night so still you could hear animals scuffling in the bushes, and the hoot of an owl was clearly audible above the murmur of the water. We were all glad of the close companionship not many yards away down the bank. At night you have no need to go searching for fish, no need of a long stretch of water. Choose your place well, and the fish will come to you, since the sea-trout are constantly heading up-stream or circling round in search of food, so even though you fish a stretch of a few yards for several hours you will never fish it out. Being so close we would call to each other when we had a pull which we failed to hook. One long eerie silence was suddenly broken as Jenks's reel gave a welcome screech. It sounded as if yards of line were being stripped off, so we hastily reeled in in order not to foul his cast as the large sea-trout raced around. Soon the reel fell quiet; we expected to hear Jenks swear at the loss of a heavy fish. His words, however, took me by surprise. 'Jasus, what in hell's that?' hardly seemed to fit the occasion, particularly when followed by 'Jasus, not again!' on a rising note of panic or anger. We listened baffled for one of Jenks's fanciful explanations of how the fish had got off. Nothing. Then a scream of 'Oh, bloody hell, Evs!'

At once we went rushing down to find out what had happened and give help as required. The intense blackness was a physical barrier on its own as we stumbled and groped our way. So anxious were we by now that one of us broke the basic rule of night fishing and shone his torch towards the river bank. The flickering beam finally settled on Jenks, looking mad but unhurt. His story flooded out: 'I was casting well across the river and almost before the fly could have landed I had a take. For a moment the line was pulled out, but then the fish seemed to lose all power and I reeled it in fast. In the dark I thought I must have a small sewin or a half-pound brown trout, so I ran my hand down the cast to release it. But it bit me – and then began flapping as well. It was a bloody bat, and when I threw the cast away to get rid of it, it simply clung on and bit me again – and then again!'

That unexpected peril of night fishing might well have panicked Jenks had he been on his own. But perhaps that might have been better for him than the ribbing he now had to endure as we gave him the dracula treatment: 'Hey, Jenks, look at the hair sprouting from your hands' from one, followed by 'Hey, Jenks, why are your teeth sticking out like that,' from another. For us it turned into one of the funniest night's fishing we had ever had, but it took Jenks some time to stop feeling sore and start sharing the joke.

Much of my early sea-trout fishing was on the Teifi River with Artie Jones as my mentor. Artie is not only an all-round angler of great ability, and a Welsh International flyfisherman, but a wonderful organiser as well. Over the years he has acquired long stretches of the Teifi for the Llandyssul Angling Club of which he has been secretary for so long. His own favourite stretch is the quiet and beautiful area where the river winds about Dolgrogws, bubbling and racing round the bends in a succession of delightful runs and glides. The daytime fishing is a joy in such surrounds, but night is when you catch the sea-trout. Artie kept reminding me of that when I ended the drive over in a fever of excitement, impatient as ever to start. 'Calm down, Gar,' Artie would say. 'You must wait until it's dark enough. No good beginning too early.'

The Teifi sea-trout did not run very large, but they were plentiful. My evenings with Artie gave me a love of this type of fishing and his personal tuition ensured that I had soon mastered the basics well enough to have some good catches. One unusual facet of Artie's night fishing is the Teifi night competition. It runs throughout the year with prizes for the largest fish caught and the best bag overall or on individual nights. The main prize is for the person who has the best record over the season. Fishermen assemble at the Half Moon Hotel for what one of them rightly described as 'a competition on the most beautiful of rivers, in the most exciting conditions against the greatest of fish'. The sensibly equipped ones will have a small torch which can be held in the mouth to leave hands free for tying on a new cast or fly while the light is pointed *away* from the river. And they will have a number of casts tied up, since at night it is much simpler to switch casts than wrestle with tangles by dim torchlight. By nine o'clock the contestants are at their chosen spot on the river bank, their bags and nets handily placed, the distance to the far bank carefully measured and a prominent landmark there imprinted on the mind.

An English visitor, John Cronin, trying this type of fishing for the first time, found it a fascinating experience: 'Don't be tempted to start too soon – not even when you hear the splash of a solid fish. When the light has faded and the bats wheel round you, then it is time to start. The river which had seemed so quiet and deserted comes suddenly to life, the still of the night broken by the screech of reels, the swish of lines, the splashing of a hooked fish, or the occasional curse as a monster is lost. For you may come that heart-stopping moment as a sewin takes, perhaps with a gentle pluck, perhaps with a savage lunge which practically wrenches the rod from your hand. In the eerie dark you will then battle with the bravest fish that swims. So absorbed will you have been by the fishing that as you finally leave for the midnight weigh-in you will be startled to find how black is the curtain of night, how disoriented and lost you can feel. Keep to the bank as the rules instruct and don't try any shortcuts. And soon there is the contrast of warmth, and light, and animated talk as the thrill of the evening is relived in the Half Moon.'

It is no surprise that Artie has been a frequent winner of the main Teifi competition, for no one has a greater love of the river or knows it better. His best catch in one short night of competition was sixteen sea-trout, but only eleven were weighed in. As he stretched to net the last he stumbled, with many fish spilling out of the bag on his back, and in the dark several drifted away on the current before he could see or retrieve them. But that was just one of the many minor mishaps likely at night, when the difficulties are so much greater, the need for care and precision so much more pronounced.

4

More Sea-Trout Memories

Most fishermen take a proper pride in the skills of the sport so when we catch fish we like to think it's entirely due to our casting ability, or our choice of fly, or our personal perception of when and where and how to work our lure. While chance and luck play a part, as in every sport, that in fact is very often true for the experienced angler. Certainly there is a special pleasure when you know you have done everything right and it has worked perfectly. So my happiest memory of sea-trout fishing is of a long summer evening and night on the Towy when I fished with textbook precision and ended with one of my best bags of these fighting fish.

The river was very low, but with many fresh-run sea-trout in the pools, a classic evening for catching them – close, warm, and cloudy. I was down there just before dusk with the freedom of the Abercothi beat, exulting in the certain knowledge that I must catch fish on such a night. With so much water to fish, and such impatience to get started, there was no need to wait for the dark. Well before the light had faded the sea-trout were moving and I was fishing the runs with a floating line and a small Stoat's Tail double, size 10. Moving quietly and with my outline merged against bank or bushes I soon had a fierce take, a wild battle, and a three-pounder successfully netted. I had to control my impulses, passing straight on to undisturbed water, otherwise after such a stimulating start I would have been dashing instead of creeping stealthily down to avoid scaring the fish. The quiet approach paid off, and in the dusk two more good fish came to the net. By now my fly was size 8; as it grew dark I changed to a sink tip and a larger Tandem fly on the point. By midnight it was changed again to a sinking line and two large Tube flies, as I searched the deep channel on Number 5 pool, the most promising night fishing spot on the beat. There I stayed for some four hours, moving only ten yards or so in that time. Every hour or two I kept changing method and fly size until by dawn I was back to size 8 and a floater.

And all through the night I was catching or losing fish, or missing some that tugged warily at the fly without any solid take. These are often the smaller ones: if a big fish decides to take it will be a firm confident rise, rather than a swift anxious snatch. There was a quick reminder of that. Soon after midnight the line checked and was held as taut as if I'd hooked a rock where no rock should be. After a moment's stillness came the explosive burst of action as a heavy fish stripped off seventy yards of line and I began stumbling blindly in pursuit over the slippery stones, part of my mind heady with excitement, part fearful of a break. Once that first rush was controlled the fight was won barring an accident, or the fouling of a snag, or a weak hook-hold, or . . . and in imagination the 'or's' multiplied. One part of my mind was saying exultantly, 'He's yours!' while the other was nervously reviewing all the possible disasters and wondering whether in the dark I would find a good place to land him. And it still seemed an eternity before the net slid under the fish at last. With a prize like that I raced many yards up the bank before switching on the torch to admire a finely proportioned sea-trout of 6½ lbs. That was the best in a bag of nine good fish. They gave me a night to remember – twelve hours of pure pleasure. Even in retrospect I can say to myself: 'I did everything right that night, just as the experts advise – and it worked a treat.' But there have been other nights, almost as good, when I have kept to just one method and rarely changed fly size, perhaps because I was feeling lazy, perhaps because I wanted to experiment, or because I found one method worked so well there was no point in changing.

As with salmon the big sea-trout often take you by surprise, coming at a place and time you least expect. That was certainly the case with the largest I've landed. On the Abercothi beat I started one evening at dusk on a shallow run which rarely held fish. I had a small Stoat's Tail on the point again and was just wetting the line preparatory to serious fishing lower down. Those first experimental casts were made where I imagined I wouldn't scare any sea-trout before the fly was sinking and working properly. At my third cast there was a big swirl and the run erupted as the great fish surged away. The fight was furious, but not unduly prolonged as it was still light enough to track the fish and play it hard. Five minutes later I was gazing in happy wonderment at an eight-pound sea-trout.

But even if some sea-trout are caught by chance and contrary to best practice or received wisdom, this type of fishing is one which rewards skill and experience more than any other. In night sea-trout fishing particularly there is a vast performance gap between the expert and the novice. On one evening the beginner may be lucky enough to catch more than the expert, just as at bridge the run of the cards may mean a couple of novices can beat Rixi Markus and Terence Reese over one rubber. But, as at bridge, experts will outscore beginners by a huge margin if they are matched over a reasonable period.

The first sea-trout of any consequence which I netted was a three-pounder on the Towy just below Llandovery. A great friend, Joe Jones, had a beat there and had given me an open invitation to fish. One warm evening I was passing on my way back home from the Royal Welsh Show in Builth Wells. As always I had my rod, a Greenheart trout rod, in the car. The water was too tempting to pass and I hurried down, catching the fish on a small Tube fly well before dark. At the time I was delirious with delight – so proud to have caught a fish this size. In retrospect I see it as a missed opportunity. The river was teeming with fish yet that was the only one I took on an ideal evening for flyfishing with the water low and sea-trout on the move. If only I had been as experienced then . . .

I was still relatively inexperienced when I hooked the biggest sea-trout of my fishing so far. Hywel Awful and I were up on the Towy above Llandeilo on the Gwaun-cum-Gurwen Club water. We had diverted from the Cothi because the river was so high and dirty. Even here it was a chuck and chance day with the rushing water giving few clues where fish might be lying. I was casting to the far bank to search as big an area as possible and soon had a good, firm take. The next ten minutes involved me in the fiercest, most spectacular of fights. Soon the fish came hurtling some four feet out of the water and a series of jumps followed between the wild rushes. Clearly it was a double figure fish. 'It's a salmon,' I said exultantly to Hywel. 'Even better,' he answered, 'it's a sea-trout. There are few salmon about now, but there are some heavy sea-trout being caught and this is clearly one of them. You can tell by the way it's playing.' Hywel was sporting his toothless grin, enjoying every moment of it. I was ashen and shaking, marvelling at the power and beauty of the fighting fish, but desperate to have him in the net. Even the cows on the opposite bank had stopped munching the grass and seemed to be gazing intently at the contest. At last I saw the gleam of him in the dark water as he turned on his side, weakening now. Hywel might have had a go at netting him as he came slowly by close in. But he held off, knowing the fish would be inert and easy to take in a few seconds more. Then the rod snapped straight, the broken line dangled tauntingly in front of me. It happened as if in slow motion; I was frozen in disbelief. For a wild moment I contemplated diving in after him. The fish was lying still only a couple of feet out and I could watch the spinner in his mouth as he sunk slowly down. As I stood indecisive he moved gently away and the bright spinner disappeared for good in the muddy water. When Hywel laughed I could have hit him. I was so disconsolate I couldn't fish again that day. My mind kept revolving the 'if onlys'. If only Hywel had tried to net him earlier, if only he had been played out seconds before, if only the line had held, for it was the metal spinner rubbing against it that had frayed and broken it. The final thought was . . . if only I had put on a stronger nylon. In high, coloured water with big fish about it pays to use 15 lb nylon rather than risk anything lighter and get broken. But that was indeed learning the lesson the cruel way.

The first essential of spinning is to be absolutely accurate in casting, so that you can put your spinner within inches of the bank or a snag without getting hooked up. That only comes with much practice. Judging depth and speed is the vital factor in presentation and that too is a matter of experience. The weight of your spinner is important in getting it to the right depth and may matter as much as size. In general I prefer lighter, smaller lures and using a fixed spool reel rather than the multiplier required for heavier ones. Fish deep and slow is standard advice for salmon; you can often work the runs by holding the rod high upstream of you and letting the spinner swing round in the current without reeling until it's near your bank. But sea-trout generally prefer a faster movement. That is one reason the Mepps does better than the Devon Minnow, which has less propulsion and glitter.

Sea-trout are best caught at night on fly, the most exciting method of all for them, but there are other ways of catching them which can also be effective and entertaining. When the water is high enough, and particularly when a breeze ruffles the surface, spinning can provide good sport: on the Towy I have often had four or five good fish in a day when I would have been unlikely to take any on fly. In low water the chances are not so good, but you may still catch them in the runs. The big sea-trout come in in April and May, when the quality is high, the quantity small – I have taken a number of five- or six-pound fish on spinner at this period. What an imposing bag a couple of brace of these make, for they are short, well-rounded fish, finely proportioned and with a bright gleam of silver. They give good sport, too, playing as well as spring salmon, and there is always the hope of a double figure fish, like that one I lost with Hywel.

By mid-June the schools of smaller fish begin to show, most of them two pounds or over but some down to half a pound. By the back-end the big ones are moving in again, but their condition now is poor: no longer do they eat well and there is little pleasure or point in catching them.

There are as many theories on the best method of spinning for Towy sea-trout as there are anglers. I have found the Mepps much the most effective, though some prefer a Devon Minnow. Size is vital to Graham Evans, who often fishes with a Mepps as small as size 1. Ken Edwards by contrast puts a size 4 Mepps on at the start of the season; the only time he changes is when he is broken and loses it, then he simply puts on another size 4 Mepps and goes on catching even in low water! As with most fishing methods it depends mainly on confidence: if you believe in what you are using, and know from your past experience that it may take fish, you will fish all the better and you will probably get the presentation right – most important of all.

If there are few salmon about, I enjoy going down to lighter rod and tackle and using 8 lb nylon, but in general it pays to fish with the maximum reasonable strength – you may meet a big fish any time and there is nothing worse than getting broken unnecessarily. With presentation so important, I find it often pays to make an angled cast upstream and bring the spinner down fast: this encourages the fish to turn and take – an entertaining sight. While you should never hammer the water there are days when your best fishing method is to spin until near dusk then change to fly, particularly true of times when the river has had a flash flood after a dry period and is fining down again. The water is ideal for spinning by day, and as it drops the evening fishing with fly may also give good sport.

You will sometimes take sea-trout when worming for salmon, but usually you need to adjust to having a single worm on the hook, if you are after sewin. When they shoal in low water there are occasions when they are embarrassingly easy to take, around dawn, by trotting down a worm to where they bunch together. It's not a form of sport which appeals to me, but I am aware of some very big bags having been taken on the Towy this way – too big, some think, when anglers have been known to take a score of sea-trout in the couple of hours after first light. In ordinary daytime worming there is, however, considerable skill in working the worm down runs with rocky bottoms. Sensibly, bubble floats are banned in our area, which makes it more demanding to swim the worm down at the right speed and depth.

The Towy is not the only Welsh river in which sea-trout run big. The Teifi has good runs of sewin, but they were more noted for numbers than size of fish. There has, however, been a recent improvement in weight, a result of more effective patrolling of the vulnerable stretch at the Cenarth Falls and a better head of fish reaching the upper waters. For big sewin the Welsh river which outshines even the Towy is the Dovey. I have long wanted to fish this river where double figure sea-trout are not uncommon, and many huge fish have been taken there in the past. One of the largest sea-trout recorded in Britain was the fish of 20 lbs 2 ozs taken from the Dovey by Mr T. Williams in 1935. They don't seem to run so large now, but one of the pleasures to which I look forward is trying to find just how large the Dovey sea-trout are today.

The Cothi has, of course, a similar run of large fish to the Towy and there is some splendid night fishing on my favourite Abercothi Beat. The Cothi became established as a great river for large sea-trout once the old Cothi Bridge Weir was destroyed and fish could then run up it freely. That was at the end of the nineteenth century; before long the owners of the upper reaches of the Towy were complaining that the main run of sea-trout turned off up the Cothi. On the Abercothi Beat we have the best of both rivers, since it includes the first mile of the Towy above the junction and the lowest reach of the Cothi. But the Cothi is some thirty miles long and I have only fished with any regularity on that bottom mile, or for trout on its headwaters. Augustus Grimble, in his well-known work on the rivers of Wales and England, particularly commended the Edwinsford Beat where he mentions one rod taking fifteen salmon, another eighteen in a few September days. That stretch was for a time one of Tony Pawson's favourites for catching big sea-trout, as he recalled to me:

'My father was a member of a group of four friends, who regularly fished the Edwinsford water. Any free weekend in summer I would leave work in London at six o'clock on a Friday and be fishing at Edwinsford before midnight. That stretch also fished well by day if you used small dry flies or size 10 wet flies, such as the Black Pennel or Black & Peacock Spider. If the water was high you caught well by day with standard patterns of sea-trout or small salmon flies, though you had little or no chance at night. Spinning was only allowed in times of flood, but even in muddy-coloured water you could take big sea-trout on a large-sized salmon fly, preferably with yellow as the dominant colour. With the chance of a fish all twenty-four hours of the day the problem was in getting any sleep. The night fishing was often at its best near dawn. The quiet time was usually midnight to 3 am and if you had to take a nap, that was the favoured period. But on the Sunday I would fish the night through, then leave just before dawn to arrive bleary-eyed at work. But even with only a few hours' sleep such weekends were a complete refreshment, with the change from work to fishing being better than a rest.

'For night fishing size 6 Alexandras or Alders were as good as any, and fished well from dark through to dawn without change of pattern or size. The longer, quieter pools were mainly at the top of the beat, the fast streams rushing through deep narrow channels mostly at the bottom towards Abernaint. The best night fishing was in the shallow tails of the main pools and often sea-trout up to seven pounds would take in a few inches of water. It is important to remember that fish see much better at night than humans and even if *you* don't notice the disturbance as a wayward cast goes in, *they* will. So rather than casting directly into the shallows at night it is better to throw the fly higher up and close to the far bank, then work it quietly down with the current. That way you avoid scaring the fish lying at the tail.

'The Edwinsford stretch has several pools which are noted for night sea-trout fishing. "The Black" was regarded as the best one to draw when several of us were fishing the river. The run at the top sidled away into a deep hole under the far bank where the water eddied round before flowing back over a shallow sandbar. That bar was a killing spot as the fish moved back and forth across it. But below was a long quiet glide where by day when the water was low you could see the sea-trout lying in ranks. At night if you moved very gently up from the bottom, wading just over ankle deep and casting straight in front, it was unusual not to move a good fish. And as long as you waded very slowly and moved very quietly you could go back to the bottom and fish it up again without having unduly disturbed the fish.

'All anglers have their special theories, which they cherish regardless of logic. Some of the group had a phobia about the porch light on the house a mile distant. Now light can have a disastrous effect at night, with a bright moon putting fish down. Car lights shining directly into the water from a road alongside, or a torch carelessly flashed into the river may also spoil the fishing (true, but odd, when you reflect that netsmen shine lights into water to *attract* fish). But a light a mile away, with intervening trees, could hardly put any off their feed. Still, that was the firm belief and we were all commanded *never* to leave the light on when anyone was fishing. Returning one night I found two colonels in angry confrontation and using language that might have made a sergeant-major blush. The aggrieved one was claiming that the other had ruined his fishing on the Black by thoughtlessly turning on the light. In a lull in the storm I made pacific noises, commiserating with him on failing to catch anything. "Caught nothing?" he bridled. "I bet I caught a damn sight more than you. I've had six and the largest is a good seven pounds. But think what I might have caught if only that idiot hadn't ruined my fishing!" There should be an interesting book to be written sometime on the "if onlys . . ." of angling.

'My own special pool was above the Black, and above the

old iron bridge now replaced by a more imposing road bridge. Dolbont had a long, fast run-in, where you could take fish at dusk without disturbing the main pool; the stream then steadied into a smooth, but narrow flow between rocks, where you might occasionally take a fish. Then it broadened into a round deep pool which tapered and shelved away into the still shallow tail which was the best at night. From Dolbont come two of my happiest memories of Cothi night fishing, and also one of the most unpleasant. The unpleasantness was of my own making, and not untypical of the hazards of fishing in the dark if you get careless. The run-in was only some eighteen inches deep under a very steep bank. In my usual impatience to start I often took a short cut, sliding down the bank in my waders. One night, as I was poised on the edge, I tripped over a piece of wire unseen in the dark, and found myself taking a long head-first dive into the trickle of water with rocks beneath. I was fortunate to escape with two sprained wrists and some cuts on the hands which broke my fall – a painful lesson on the need for careful movement at night.

'That caution has never quite extended to my driving when late for fishing. The prelude to my best night on Dolbont was reporting a West Indies *v* Glamorgan cricket match at Swansea and telephoning my final copy later than I had intended. The Edwinsford housekeeper had asked me to give a lift back to her brother, who had also been at the match. In the circumstances I thought my driving was well-controlled, if a bit swift, but when I let him out he appeared rather white and shaky. The housekeeper told me that when I appeared briefly on a television programme he was watching, some months later, he grabbed her hand and said, "Jasus, woman, don't say that madman is *still* alive." The fish, anyway, were very much alive that summer night, taking firmly and steadily throughout. Just after midnight the line went taut and immovable as a heavy fish hooked on. For what seemed an eternity it stayed as still as the night. Then for ten minutes it cruised quietly round the bottom of the pool, unhurried and apparently unworried. Finally it decided the game had gone on long enough, and set off upstream. There was no rush, no screaming reel, just a steady majestic progress, silent and unseen. Through the round pool it went, through the narrow channel, and on up the run-in, as I scrambled in pursuit, vainly trying to check it. Suddenly the hold gave, the line went slack. Was it the largest sea-trout I had ever hooked or a salmon, more of which are caught at night than theory would have us believe? Even without that prize to top it off the night yielded nine fish, the largest five pounds. There should still have been the dawn fishing to come, but before it I had to head off reluctantly to take part in a charity cricket match in London, thinking of the fish I was missing.

'That early morning period can be the most productive of all. After one long unsuccessful night I began to fish the tail of Dolbont in the hour before dawn. It seemed quiet and dead. Then heavy rain came splattering down and for a couple of hours the fish went crazy. They were taking not as at night, in the tail, but in the deeper middle water. Nor, unfortunately, were they taking as firmly as they do at night, with many coming short or plucking at the fly or swirling round it. But with a rise almost every other cast, enough hooked on for a blank to have become a bag of a dozen by breakfast.

'A sudden change in atmospheric conditions can have electrifying effect on salmon and sea-trout. Another good Edwinsford pool was Oak Tree, with its run-in divided by a rock outcrop and a wide area of quiet water below. The river had been low for weeks, the fish torpid by day, and no salmon had moved, even to the weighted Tube flies which often took them in the deep gutters below Oak Tree Pool. In the clear water I could see lines of sea-trout and many salmon lying listless and inert. Neither wet nor dry fly stirred a fish. Then the wind got up, the sky darkened and soon a thunderstorm was centred over the Cothi. For the half hour it lasted the whole of Oak Tree boiled with rampaging fish. Two salmon were landed and one lost before the storm moved on and the fish sank back to the old passive indifference.

'Only two other places I have fished have rivalled that beat of the Cothi for large sea-trout. Loch Stack in Sutherland used to have great runs of big sea-trout coming in up the Laxford River, famous for that picture of a mosquito-netted Neville Chamberlain absorbed in fishing while the world waited breathless on the brink of war. The first time I fished Stack I had two sea-trout weighing fifteen pounds between them, caught on that invaluable all-round fly, the Black Pennel. My wife had a six-pounder, too, while dapping. The keen young gillie had kept saying to her: "Any minute now something like a barn door will erupt from the water." A big fish rising to a large dapping fly is indeed a spectacular sight, and when the "barn door" surged up I was surprised she was restrained enough to follow the earlier advice to say "God save the Queen" before striking. Too much netting has reduced Stack now to an ordinary sea-trout and salmon loch, with limited numbers of large sea-trout. They are of a Norwegian strain, and that is where there is matchless fishing for these monsters. The Laerdal River in Norway there has given me the most exciting sea-trout fishing of all. On its lowest beat the river is wide, the water crystal clear. By day you can fish dry fly with imitations of the Bibio Pomona, or any small black fly, giving you a chance to watch one of these great fish rise purposefully from the bottom. Once, while I was there, a young Norwegian, Einar Wahlstrom, took a record sea-trout in the afternoon, fishing downstream with a size 10 Butcher. It took him an hour to land and weighed just over twenty-five pounds!

'But for me the real delight was the night fishing. Mountains enclosed the river, looming so steep and sheer that for months in winter the sun never reaches the valley floor. But when I fished in August it was never really dark; even at midnight there was a soft luminous light like dusk on a warm summer evening in England. The current was fast, the pools long, and fishing with streamer flies there was a near certainty of big sea-trout. When they took they would race away down the heavy stream in spectacular rushes that took you far down river. Thirteen pounds was the largest I had among numerous double figure fish.

'Yet sheer size is not the only criterion. Where the average run is small then a large fish caught bulks proportionately bigger in your own mind. My most memorable sea-trout was one taken in August in the Erriff River in Connemara. The river is not noted for big sea-trout, though it has a huge run of small 'harvesters' at this time, and you might catch a score of pounders in a day. In a favourite pool on the Upper Erriff, Derryherbert, I hooked what I took to be a grilse in the exact spot where as a ten-year-old I had caught my first salmon. But when netted it turned out to be the largest sea-trout taken in that river for many years. It weighed over six pounds and the water keeper was so excited by it that some of its scales were sent off to the Irish Specimen Fish Committee in Dublin. Palmists may guess at your destiny by reading the lines in your hand, but the scientists can go much better than that by telling you a fish's life history from just a few scales. I still treasure the report from the Department, signed by A. E. J. Went: "The fish was definitely a sea-trout just over seven years old. It had spent three years in freshwater before going to sea as a smolt and another three years in the sea before returning to freshwater in 1965. It had spawned in that spawning season, returned to the sea to recover and had made its way back to freshwater shortly before capture."

'A peculiar difference of the Irish West Coast rivers is that sea-trout fishing is much better by day than night, even when the water is low. On the Erriff all you need is a breeze to ruffle the surface of the many long quiet pools and there are plenty of fish for the taking, even in a drought. The killing combination of flies for me on such waters is a Connemara Black and a Black Pennel – and it doesn't matter too much which is the dropper. In low water size 10 or 12 are the most effective, with size 8 adequate on a high but clearing river. These small flies are just as likely to catch you a salmon, too. That indeed is my ideal of day fishing – good prospects of sea-trout, with the chance of the occasional salmon. The specimen sea-trout took a size 10 Black Pennel, reminding again that it's not necessary to fish with big flies to catch big fish.'

For daytime fishing on the Cothi, as on the Towy, spinning is often the most productive method. Casting across and up-stream is one of the most effective methods for many of the pools. But however and wherever you try for sea-trout, this great fish will give you unrivalled sport.

5

The Lure of the Salmon

How fortunate I was that it took me so long to catch my first salmon. Expectation denied and hope deferred merely heightened my sense of anticipation, making the prize even more desirable. The more intense, then, was my feeling of achievement when at last one of those great fish lay glistening at my feet. The greater, too, was my respect – reverence, even – for the salmon which had proved so hard to catch: waiting had enriched the moment of triumph.

That early enchantment has never changed. No matter the many blank days, no matter the frequent frustrations, this is the kind of fishing which has special and lasting fascination for me. In a recent season, when I was up on the River Dee, the gillie recounted with wonder his experience with a novice fisherwoman. She had learnt to spin but this was her first day's salmon fishing. It coincided with a memorable run of fish through her beat and, inexperienced as she was, she still had the kind of catch which remains for many just a lifelong dream. By lunch she had landed six salmon from twelve to twenty-two pounds. 'How boringly easy,' was her only reaction. 'I'm off home, and won't bother to come salmon fishing again.'

Having learnt the hard way there is never any danger of my becoming surfeited with the sport. Though I have now caught a fair number of salmon, there seems always something unusual, something unique, about each capture – the way the fish took suddenly on a hopeless-looking day, or the way it fought, or how it nearly snagged me, or how big it was, or how strong and lively, or how beautifully proportioned – most salmon leave some special impression on the mind. Recall of many of them is easy but that first one – that's indelibly etched on my memory. It was February and I was spinning on the Usk. The water was high and coloured and there was no expectation that many fish were running. Suddenly came that heart-stopping moment of the heavy, solid take followed by the first fierce rush of a springer. The ten-minute battle seemed to last ten years, with anxiety overlaying anticipation, especially in those final moments as the fish swirled and splashed at the sight of the net. When my friend lifted it out, elation was boundless. The fish was a finely shaped hen of eleven pounds, the most beautiful sight on which my eyes had ever lighted. I could have kissed that salmon in my excitement and by the time I had finished showing it round to all my acquaintances it must have shrunk to half its original weight.

The point in the river where it was hooked is within sight of the Newport to Monmouth road, down which I often travel. As I drive past I always glance down to that spot, and the occasion, the time, the fish, come vividly to mind. Equally fresh in memory is the first salmon I landed on my own without a friend to advise or assist. The river was the Usk again, the pool long and deep, curving round a bend. In those days I carried an inefficient tailer, rather than the net I now take slung whenever I go salmon fishing. Hardly had I struck home than I realised the tailer was left at the head of the pool some eighty yards distant.

With that realisation came blind panic. On the opposite bank I saw the keeper's dog and, assuming incorrectly that his master must be close at hand, I kept yelling for him to come and help me. It never occurred to me to wonder what possible aid he could give me from across the river. When it was clear he was not within earshot, and I was indeed on my own, panic still blinded me to the obvious solution. Now I would simply walk the salmon, moving steadily and without reeling. Then I edged back all those eighty yards, cautiously letting out line and praying the fish wouldn't move. By the time I reached the tailer I was well into the backing and had the fish been active it would certainly have broken me. Mercifully it stayed quiet, no doubt as bemused as I was. That salmon weighed some seventeen pounds, and for me everything about it remains unforgettable.

You can learn a lot about salmon fishing from reading, and much more from listening to, and watching, expert friends, but the lessons of experience are more quickly and lastingly absorbed. That applies particularly to the playing of fish. Games players like myself start with the advantage of a highly developed sense of touch and quick reactions but, as in so much of this sport, the most important and interesting aspect is learning to think like the fish, to anticipate what it may do. To be able to play salmon hard, but not so hard that you are broken by the unexpected run, or the sideways leap, or the final plunge, comes from observed experience sensibly recorded in the mind.

Mastering the unusual hazards is more difficult. One early success came when I was fishing with one of my closest friends, Graham Evans, on his beat of the Towy. The best taking place in the pool started where two old tree stumps angled up a few feet out of the water. Clearly their roots were much closer to me as I fished down, but the exact position was hard to judge. As always with his guests, Graham had invited me to fish down first and was following on some twenty yards behind. 'There's a good chance of a fish lying just above the tree roots, Gareth,' he called to me as I neared the spot. It was a peculiar thrill, therefore, to cast the minnow accurately enough to sweep just in front of the snag and then feel the solid pull of a good fish. A very lively one it was too, and before I could come to terms with it the salmon had dashed down the far side of the stumps. I checked it before it had gone much further, but I couldn't work it back against the current. As I tried part of the line was soon lying across the stump and a break seemed inevitable. 'Let the line out, Gareth,' said Graham, 'then I'll try and catch the bottom length with my spinner, recover it, tie it on my rod and you can play it then from a different position clear of the obstruction.' It sounded like *Mission Impossible*, but at least it was better than staying anchored this way until the line parted. Graham duly caught the belly of line and drew it over without exciting the salmon. Then came the desperate moment of cutting my line and tying it on to his. He assured me the salmon would stay quiet, but every second I was expecting the line to be ripped from my hand as I fumbled anxiously with the knot. I hadn't caught many salmon then and couldn't bear the thought of losing this one with the hazard so nearly overcome. But the fish stayed quiet, the new knot held and a fourteen-pounder was soon netted, thanks to the experienced Graham's ingenuity. When you're about to fish a place with a snag like this, it pays to work out in advance exactly what you will do when you hook a fish in order to avoid trouble as you deal with it.

Had I lost that salmon at that stage of my fishing career it would have ruined my day. For years the loss of a good fish left me desolate – it was always the lost fish that haunted the mind rather than those brought to the net. At least the acute disappointment is a measure of how committed you are to your fishing and how much it means to you, but to enjoy it to the full you need to come to terms with such misfortune. Some losses are inevitable, however faultless your playing. Now I can accept them with equanimity – after an initial moment of despair as the line goes slack.

After such a fight I can even identify with the fish and feel that his courage deservedly won him his freedom; and my reaction to a similar misfortune in a recent season was certainly not gloom. I was fishing on a warm summer night, the gentle lap of the water the only sound in the dark. Suddenly all was confusion and echoing noise: the line was torn out and a great sea-trout or salmon splashed luminously on the surface. It was a memorable combat, with the wild surges of the fish all the more testing in the blindness of the night. At last he was beaten and I saw the gleam of him as he turned on his side close to my feet. Keeping the tension, with my small single-handed rod held high and arched under the strain, I waded in to net him. Probably this was another monster Towy sea-trout but it might be a salmon, taking at night as the occasional one does, for despite maximum strain on the rod I could not move him now – the line was taut and unyielding. Wearying of the stalemate, I ran my hand down the cast to see if I could shake him into life; just below the surface it banged against rock. His fierce strength hadn't thrown me, so he'd beaten me by stealth: as I waded out he'd circled the rock, twisted my cast round it and effortlessly snapped off the fly. It pleased me that this had been just a small Hairy Mary, which would cause him little inconvenience. After the first bitter realisation that he was gone I was able to take my cap off to him and feel grateful for the thrill of that battle, the pleasure of a demanding contest in which he had finally outwitted me. Almost I credited him with intelligence, rather than instinct, which had won him survival.

The first thing to learn about salmon is that they are quite unpredictable. No one can tell you why a fish which does not feed in fresh water as it runs upriver to spawn should take a variety of lures from a worm to a dry fly. No one can tell you for certain that you will catch one, however promising the day looks. And happily no one can tell you you *won't* catch one, however slim the prospect. Salmon are masters of the unexpected and that's why it's always worth having a try for them. That first salmon I caught on my own on the Usk had come out of the blue. I hadn't meant to go fishing, but to get my passport. 'You've two hours to wait,' I was told, 'so why not have a cup of tea?' Instead I slipped down to the river for something to do, with no thought that I might catch a salmon in the brief time I could spare on the bank.

It was the same with Graham Evans. He was teaching his son to spin with a small six-foot rod, 7 lb nylon, and a size 1 Mepps, in low water with little prospect of a fish. He had reeled up for the last time, but his son kept asking him to show him a back cast. 'Well, just once,' said Graham finally, before flicking out the small minnow. Immediately it was seized by a heavy fish and after a long wearing fight he landed his largest salmon – 31½ lbs. You can theorise as much as you like, but in salmon fishing there is no such thing as the right way. Graham is very expert on the Towy and adapts his fishing to the state of the water. At the start of the season, when it is high and coloured, he will be using a size 4 Mepps or a Devon Minnow and 18 lb nylon. By midsummer he will be down to 7 lb and size 1. Ken Edwards is at least as expert and knows everything about the river, so you expect him to use that knowledge to make fine adjustments of lure and tackle. He too starts the season with a size 4 Mepps and heavy nylon. On a fine midsummer day that will still be on his rod, and his tackle will be unchanged at the back-end. And Ken will have caught as many salmon as anyone.

With such big and sporting fish you can't predict what will happen to you either. There is a pool on the Towy where the water glides over a weir at the tail. Fishing down towards it on one occasion the rod was nearly jerked from my hands as a salmon smashed into my spinner. Down over the weir it went, in its first unstoppable rush. With the rod hooped under the massive strain I gradually pumped him back, but each time I worked him near, off he would go again and the laborious struggle was renewed as I wound him carefully in against the heavy current. It was a long time before he gave in, turning on his side as I reached for the net. Then my rod tip cracked under the relentless pressure. For a moment, as the rod splintered, I froze in shock. With the salmon drifting away on the current I then risked everything by grabbing the line and handlining the salmon in before it could recover. Fortunately it was played out and came quietly – a fine fish of 14½ lbs with the sea-lice still on him. The elation of landing that fish made up for the loss of the rod and the rest of the day's fishing.

I was amused, too, that the handlining stirred memories of an hilarious encounter on the Dee. It was on one of the most prestigious beats, where the gillies were used to looking after more cultured anglers who were able fishermen and genteel of manner. Invited with me was Harry, who was neither.

While I flyfished down a beautiful run under the gillie's eye, Harry disappeared with the spinning rod which he professed to have little knowledge of using. My fly searched the water meticulously, the current swinging it invitingly over the best lies. Nothing moved to it all morning. As we broke for lunch Harry came back whistling, with a wraith-like salmon dangling over one arm. In condition it would have weighed over 15 lb, but the gillie had a sharp intake of breath when he saw it. 'A kelt. You mus'na keep kelts,' he said sternly. 'So that's what it is!' said Harry, looking blank. 'Perhaps the other was a salmon.' 'What other?' I asked him. 'It was longer than this and much fatter. Very silvery it looked. A real tug-of-war I had with him. He nearly pulled the rod out of my hands so I took hold of the cord and dragged him on to the bank. Very hard on my hands it was. And the fish was only part way up the bank when the hook came out. He went flapping and bouncing back to the river, even though I kept hitting him on the head with my rod to stop him. It hasn't done the rod much good, but didn't seem to worry him.' I was doubled up listening, the gillie left speechless. I don't think Harry has been invited back.

Because salmon can be so unpredictable chance often plays a greater part in their capture than is normal with other game fish but there's no question of salmon fishing being a matter of chuck and hope. There are so many skills involved and a vast discrepancy in the numbers caught in a season by the expert and by the average angler. Two qualities, however, are essential for all those who want to be good at the sport – patience and perseverance. No matter how competent you are, blank days are unavoidable, periods of disappointment inevitable. Yet once caught by salmon fishing's special fascination even these can be enjoyable if you are patient and dedicated. Izaak Walton was no salmon fisherman, but he caught the mood when he wrote of a day on which he caught nothing: 'The angling has been so pleasant it has proved to be, like virtue, a reward in itself.' I can think of no other sport which I can genuinely enjoy when I have no success at all. Salmon fishing can keep me totally absorbed, totally happy, however vain the pursuit may prove. There is no pleasure to equal flyfishing for salmon on a river suited for it, but I'm glad that I was taught to enjoy a variety of methods for, as with so many others, much of my salmon fishing is on rivers where flyfishing gives little hope of success at many periods of the season. It's fine to be a fly-only addict if you have permanent access to the best of Scottish rivers, but to enjoy your fishing in a variety of rivers you need to master a variety of techniques.

It was my good fortune to be taught by two highly experienced fishermen, each passionately devoted to a different method of catching salmon. Artie Jones was the wizard of the worm, bringing a high level of skill to an often despised form of fishing. Jack Jones was devoted to flyfishing, and very knowledgeable in the art. Both of them could take fish spinning, worming, or flyfishing and with their different specialities they made ideal teachers. Each respected the other's particular skill and in one way at least they complemented each other. As Artie puts it: 'If Jack or anyone else moves a salmon on a fly and can't get it to take, then I'm certain to catch it if they let me have a go with a worm.'

More often, though, it was Jack, who, coming down after Artie and I had spun and wormed the pools, would still take a fish. He was a quiet friendly man, and a deliberate and methodical angler. He too had a firm belief that how you presented the fly was more important than the fly you presented. The same two were always on his cast – a Logie on the tail and a Blue Charm as dropper. Many ignore a dropper when fishing for salmon because of the problems it may bring: if you hook the fish on the dropper the tail fly may snag as it trails behind in the fight; if the fish takes the tail fly there's less chance of snagging, but the cast is weakened anyway by the dropper knot and may still break there. And occasionally a sea-trout may seize the dropper as the salmon takes it down deep, and to have another fish on doesn't help in landing the salmon. But Jack caught a lot of fish on his dropper and very rarely lost one.

Artie is a good enough flyfisherman to have been in the Welsh International team, but his real expertise is with a worm and it fascinates me still to watch him. Those who think worming is a matter of chuck and chance should see him in action. He is a perfectionist, forever making minor adjustments to his weights and to how he swims the worm. Artie aims always to have it down where the salmon are, moving naturally along at the pace of the current. The constant fiddling and changing amused me when first I went out with him and I thought it just affectation and a waste of time. When I asked him about it his answer made me understand for the first time the most essential principle of any form of fishing: 'It's a question of presentation, Gareth. Fish won't take unless you present the bait right. Why should they? If you get a greasy plate of food shoved at you in a café your appetite goes quickly enough. But if it's made to look nice, with all the trimmings and pleasantly served, then you'll tuck in eagerly enough. Fish aren't any different in preferring their food properly presented. And with salmon more than any other fish it's up to you to attract them. They don't feed naturally in rivers. They aren't hunting for food all the time. But place a tasty morsel gently in front of their nose and they may swallow it. Chuck it at them and you haven't a chance.'

That was an early lesson which has stuck with me. Well – two lessons, really, and both fundamental to any form of fishing. Concentrate on presenting the worm or the fly or the spinner as attractively as possible. And concentrate also on trying to understand how fish react and what motivates them to take. Then, like Artie with his worms, you'll find added interest and have much greater success as you become able to work out for yourself where fish are likely to be and what form of presentation is likely to entice them. When I'm worming for salmon I follow Artie's precepts in the main: 'Keep searching all the time. Don't let the worm lie at the end of each cast as some do, spending ten minutes or so ledgering before they cast again. Wait just a moment, then trot the worm down again. Adjust the weights and mend the line so that you're always in control of the speed at which the worm travels. Make it go at the pace of the water. Learn the likely lies and search them carefully. Learn the depths of the water and keep your worms down near the bottom.'

Artie has many little devices to make his fishing simpler and more precise. His weights are like folded lead washers, easy to slip on. Then he twists them so that they don't snag as often as they would if left flat. And when they *do* snag he has a technique for that too: 'Whether you get snagged in a rock or a tree, with a fly, a worm or a spinner, there is one simple method which gives you the best chance of recovering your tackle intact. DON'T start yanking the rod, whatever you do. As soon as you sense you're snagged let the rod drop and pick up the line. Then pull it in gently until it is just taut. Now give a series of short steady pulls until it comes free. Four times out of five it will.'

However expert your teacher, the method that suits him best may not be ideal for you. Part of the fun of fishing is working things out for yourself. As with learning to write, you start by copying the pothooks the teacher puts before you, but having begun from the same basic method as all other children you go on soon to develop your own distinctive style. Much of what Artie showed me is still part of my fishing technique, but in many ways I have adapted as other ideas have appealed to me. So it is with weights when worming. I don't use Artie's type, I use little metal balls suspended from the cast, which are round and even less likely to snag. And if they do all you lose is the weight, not the rest of your tackle.

The sport never stales once you appreciate the need to think through the many variables, to try and arrive at a form of presentation that the fish will find most palatable. Many factors are important in that – the lure itself can be crucial, whether it be fly, spinner or worm. That, too, Artie taught me. Nothing is left to chance with his worms. His own wormery is fashioned and maintained in his garden with loving care, so before he goes to the river he can take his pick from worms developed to prime conditions by his own special formula. This is Artie's method: 'Use only garden worms dug up in early spring. Put them in a barrel with layers of earth. Add soured milk and oats at intervals. Keep moist newspaper on top and ensure it's kept damp at regular intervals. Put a protective cover on it and there will be a supply of toughened worms ready to hand all season.'

Flyfishing has attracted me more than other methods. Each method requires its own special skills and brings its own satisfactions, and I'm grateful to Bryn Evans for teaching me so much about spinning, and to Artie for letting me into the secrets of worming. But flyfishing has been the main attraction for me. The casting action, the precise placement of the fly, the working of it in stream or slack give pleasure in themselves, quite apart from catching fish. And when the fish do take the rise is more exciting to fly, and there is more skill required in the hooking. So Jack Jones – 'Alma' as we called him, after the shoe shop he ran – was also a major influence in my fishing education. He was as addicted to fly as Artie to his worms, and the two would argue fiercely the merits of their own specialities, while I was content to absorb it all.

From Jack 'Alma' I learned the sizes and dressings of flies most likely to take fish on Usk, Cothi, Towy and of course on his beloved Teifi. He taught me dodges like fishing for sea-trout with a Tandem fly on the point and a Tube fly as dropper and how to work them just above the algae. Jack liked to see me cast at an angle of 45 degrees, disliked wading if it could be avoided and advised going down a pool slowly, but keeping on the move – some two feet down after each couple of casts. From Jack, as from Artie and Bryn, came the soundest advice to launch me as a salmon and sea-trout fisherman. The rest was up to me as experience and experiment improved my confidence and widened my range.

6

My Favourite Rivers

Fishing takes you to places which are a joy to the eye, a refreshment to the spirit. So many lakes and rivers have left pleasant pictures on my mind. I can look at waters like Blagdon or Chew and appreciate their beauty; the broad majestic salmon rivers of Scotland have their charm, as do many of Wales's swift and sparkling streams. But there is one place which has no rival in my heart. If in rugby Cardiff Arms Park was my spiritual home, in fishing the place where I am totally fulfilled, completely at ease, is just one stretch of the River Towy where it joins the Cothi. Some lines of Kipling's exactly express its attraction for me:

> Go softly by that riverside
> Or when you would depart
> You'll find its every winding
> Tied and knotted round your heart.

Many are the waters which I admire and enjoy, but there is only one I love. Most anglers know such an enchanted place, their ideal which no other can match. We may not want our ashes scattered there, as Skues willed his own to be beside his beloved Itchen, but in life its hold on us is complete. For me the Abercothi stretch of the Towy is this ideal. It has everything my angler's heart can desire. There's a nice contrast of scenery, with lush pastures on one bank, thick woodland on the other. On both there is a quiet peace, isolating you from the noise and cares of the world. The Towy here is a broad, serene river, more sedate than the bubbling effervescent Teifi, another of my loves, but with a wide variety of pace and mood, a series of pools of different character and challenge. At any height of water and at any time of day or night there are places where you may hope to take a salmon or a sea-trout. At the bottom of the beat it's joined by the shallower, narrower, more rapid waters of the Cothi, providing another change, another mile or two of prime sea-trout fishing. Those who come regularly to Abercothi are a friendly group, complementing the pleasure, as does Ken Edwards, who understandably has a fund of knowledge, a wealth of helpful advice.

For one, like myself, brought up as an all-round fisherman, the pools provide opportunity to flyfish, spin, or worm, with favoured spots for each method. Familiarity with this water breeds nothing but contentment with so wide a variety of choice, so many places to fish with expectation. At the top is the long quiet reach, called 'Sir John', good for spinning in high water, but the most promising area comes as it tails off into the 'Pigstye', where the bank is steeply cut away below the farm buildings. Here the fish rest as they come up from the Abercothi run. That run is mainly channelled into a deep hole on the far bank. If there's a taking salmon there, it may fall to any of the three methods. Often you may have no success with fly, no movement to a spinner, and then catch it on the worm. And a demanding place it is for worm fishing – you need to work the worm past the many snags just below the surface of the stream before sinking it down into the deep water at the head, where a fish will most likely be lying.

Below the run the river broadens out into a long pool of gentle current. The holding places change with the years in this interesting mixture of dead water and good lies. Currently the middle section, with its clumps of weed and its glide past the overhang of trees on the far bank, is the most hopeful place, if there is enough water. It was here that I took my largest salmon from the beat, a hard-fighting fish of 21½ lbs.

The river's height is not controlled solely by rainfall: on the Towy's upper reaches is a dam, which many blame for a decline in the quantity of fish in the river. A release of water from the dam may provide a sudden freshet, a rise of several inches, when the river is low and stagnant. But that is not unmixed gain, for the flow pours out from the bottom of the dam where the temperature is very low, and the sudden surge of cold water is as likely to put fish down as to encourage them to take. Runs of salmon and large sea-trout are still plentiful, but they don't match earlier times when anglers spoke of the 'blue cloud' of shoaling sea-trout. In Ken Edward's mind the villain is not the dam, but the now 'protected' cormorant. His obsession about the damage these birds cause is not blind prejudice, but based on a study of their habits and on his own personal experience in his early days on the water: 'The Water Authority chief then blamed a fall-off in the runs of fish on the profusion of cormorants. He used to encourage us to shoot them, with an offer of half-a-crown a head. As a result we had a real purge of the cormorants and there was soon a very marked improvement in fish stocks. The cormorants come up from the coast from winter through to spring, and the small parr become their main target in the cold barren waters. In one diving session a cormorant has been found to swallow over thirty parr, and they are unbelievably rapacious and destructive.'

Below the Abercothi Pool the river changes character, with a number of swift runs, many with deep channels cut through the slanting, slippery rock. To fish some you can wade out on old concrete drums, while at Number 3 Pool there is an L-shaped pier standing proud above the lap of water unless the river is in flood. This is a fascinating place to fish with a spinner. Casting up above from the pier and reeling in fast often brings fish in the rush at the head. Level with the pier the water swirls by in circling eddies, difficult to fish. The spinner has to be worked deep then drawn up, and the salmon takes with a sudden explosive dart as it comes near the surface. That's a heart-stopping moment and the memory of past encounters keeps you tense and expectant as you fish it down. Below are the best sea-trout runs, though the rocks make

Two beautiful silver fish taken on Gordon's Fancy in November on the Tweed.

Some participants in the annual House of Commons *v* the Salmon and Trout Association match. Left to right: Roger Daltry, Bernard Cribbins, Peter Tombleson, Ted Northcote, Sir Geoffrey Johnson-Smith MP and Cranley Onslow MP, with Tony Pawson in the background.

Wading at The Grain, the bottom end of the Junction Beat on the Tweed.

Billy and I are delighted with our morning's catch on the Bridge Pool at the Junction Beat.

wading treacherous at night until you know it so well that the contours are etched on your memory. Where the Cothi flows quietly in there's a glide close to the bank at the extreme end of the beat. Often the fish shoal there, waiting to move into the Cothi, so it can provide exciting sport in the dark. Fishing on your own in the still of the night you can often see torches moving on the beat downstream and hear low voices echo clearly over the water as anglers below tell each other of their catch. The Cothi's own Junction Pool is another favourite place, for in low water it often has sea-trout lying in ranks as they wait to move upstream to the many holding areas where the river winds away to the distant road bridge. Part of the pleasure of fishing a familiar and well-loved river is in the special associations that each pool has. Even if the fish are quiet, memory may be active.

All along the Abercothi beat there are places where you may take fish, but the catching of fish – or the hope of catching fish – is only a part of its charm for me. Equally important is the companionship of others who fish there and of Ken Edwards. No one intrudes when you are in solitary mood, but more often you are only too ready to enjoy the exchange of advice and banter. It's pleasant to know other fishermen on the beat so well that you can guess where and how they will fish. Recently I was alerted to a freshet of water coming from the dam after a barren period of drought. A worm in the Abercothi run appeared a good chance, as I hurried down in hopes of a salmon. There was just one car at the park when I arrived; I knew instantly who it was and that he would almost certainly have the same idea. So before fishing the run I looked carefully round. There on the stones were the telltale scales where a salmon had recently been landed, so instead of wasting time worming there I changed to fly, went down to the run in Number 3 and was soon playing a lively salmon.

When Graham Evans or other special friends are present there's always friendly rivalry which makes each of us fish that much harder. There's a readiness, too, to indulge in the occasional leg-pull, which keeps us alert. When we meet up after several hours' fishing we enquire eagerly if the other has caught anything. The bland 'Nothing' is always suspect, and we scrutinise the speaker carefully. As often as not he'll have a fish scale or two on his glasses or his forehead to tell us the real answer, if we can read the sign aright. Then off we dash to have a look at the fish we know he's caught. On one occasion after Graham and I had both denied catching anything we noticed simultaneously the scales each had on him. 'When did you catch it?' I asked. 'I hooked it at eight o'clock precisely,' Graham replied. 'Odd,' I answered. 'I checked my watch too as I hooked mine and it was that exact minute. What weight was yours?' 'Eight pounds to the ounce.' Curiouser and curiouser, for mine was also eight pounds to the ounce. 'What fly?' 'Size 6 Stoat's Tail,' said Graham, and by some remarkable coincidence his catch duplicated mine in every particular. An ordinary fish suddenly became a remarkable one through a fishing friendship. 'You can't measure the pleasure by the catch' is an apt enough saying. Sharing an experience so often heightens it, or even turns a blank day into a memorable one.

Graham's own water, higher up the Towy at Golden Grove, also has a special attraction for me. As with Abercothi, its two-mile stretch is notable for the variety of water and of challenge to the angler. As with Abercothi, too, many of its pools have the power to evoke a memory, recalling for me moments of exhilaration, despair or humour. On one my mind goes back to a mild summer day when my No 6 Hairy Mary was seized by a salmon. Many stay quiet and still at first, or shake their heads as if disbelieving that they are hooked. Not this one. He was off like a powerboat, stripping out some sixty yards of line with effortless ease. Then he shot high into the air. Even from a distance he looked over twenty-five pounds, so he may well have been around thirty! A high jump will usually exhaust so large a fish, but this one just kept going. Then the cast snapped, leaving me desolate. Failure to check and remove a knot in the cast had cost me the biggest salmon I've hooked on the Towy. The tremendous strain exerted not by the rod, but by the length of trailing line had searched out the weakness. Lessons are useful, but again that was a cruel way to learn. As I look at the pool today, the ache of that moment is fierce still.

Sometimes I rest in the shade of trees by another pool there, recalling one of the many successful practical jokes played by Phil Bennett's father-in-law, Les Jones. Graham had caught a small salmon and we sat there admiring it. As we talked, Les idly pressed some small stones into its vent. No doubt he had some plan to disconcert Graham later, but he could not have foreseen the result. Graham, as usual, sent the fish to the freezer and as usual had it later cut into chunks by a bandsaw. But the pebbles broke the blade of the saw and Graham was mystified until he spotted them. Next day he was full of his discovery. 'Did you know salmon eat stones?' he kept asking. 'My last one was full of them.' We had difficulty containing ourselves and of course the culprit wasn't going to say anything now that the saw was broken. The more we dismissed the idea, the more assertive Graham became, until finally Les confessed. Graham was not as amused as the rest of us. A local farmer was caught out later in much the same way. Passing one of his moletraps, an angler slipped in a small sea-trout to find the reaction. Those who will listen are still being told in the pub that the farmer knows sea-trout can also travel overland. How else would one have ended in his trap?

The Teifi is another river which has the happiest memories for me, rating close to the Cothi and Towy in my affection. It is a clear, fast stream with plenty of weedbanks in the higher reaches where I've had some good brown trout fishing. But it is the waters of the Llandyssul Angling Association which have provided me with the best sport and also with a special privilege and a particular pride. Artie Jones had introduced me to night sea-trout fishing there and after the successful Lions tour of 1971 he made me an honorary member of the Association for five years 'to give back a little of the satisfaction you and the Lions gave us'. But not satisfaction for everyone apparently. It's rare for all fishermen to agree on anything and apparently one or two members promptly resigned 'because the honour went to a rugby player and no one has given a similar privilege to great soccer players like John Charles'. I was overjoyed when Artie told me I had been given the freedom of the Association's waters which, under his expert guidance, now stretch for over sixteen miles. It saddened me later to hear of the defections caused by a kind gesture which I so much appreciated, but certainly they were the losers for their somewhat unsporting reaction – the Llandyssul Association has such splendid fishing and in the main such friendly fishermen.

Poaching is a danger everywhere these days but it's difficult on the well-fished waters of the Llandyssul Association for, as I found, an MI5-type network operates effectively there. You don't get far unnoticed! My wife, Maureen, and I had an amusing demonstration of this when we were on honeymoon. My great friend, Cliff Morgan, had been very ill and I got a message that he would be down on the Teifi with David Coleman. We were due to motor past the Teifi, but where on all its long reach they might be, I had no idea. Eager to see Cliff, I called in hopefully at the small local police station and felt a little foolish asking the constable if he knew where Cliff was. 'Just a moment, sir,' he said cheerfully. 'We heard a rumour he was here. I'll ask around and find out.'

There was no 'perhaps I'll find him'! It needed only a couple of calls before I was told the exact pool where I could find them if I hurried. My arrival on the riverbank was perfectly timed from my point of view. David Coleman was doing his best to extricate some twenty yards of his line which he had wrapped round overhanging branches. The suave commentator had to put up with facetious questions on whether he thought he could catch salmon up trees. Cliff enjoyed the banter and I was delighted to find him fully recovered. Apart from our close association on the rugby field he had been the first television personality interested enough in fishing to interview me about my passion for the sport, and it was partly through that television programme that my friendship started with Clive

Gammon, who was later to involve me in the most gruelling few days' fishing of my life.

Maureen was beginning to learn the hard way what it means to be married to a fisherman. We were only on the road to our honeymoon hotel and already I had found a good excuse to divert to the riverside. There was, needless to say, a rod in the back of the car and I had been careful to choose an hotel with a small stream flowing past it. Several mornings I crept down in the dawn to have a try for sea-trout before breakfast, leaving the rest of the day for expeditions with Maureen. The hotel proprietor was a keen fisherman, too. One morning he told me he was going to fish the sea pool of the Mawddach, and invited me to come too. It was a tempting offer, and at a propitious moment I cleared my throat and suggested to Maureen that perhaps a trip to the mouth of the Mawddach had more to offer than the planned visit to Barmouth. Despite my enthusiastic description of the scenery and the pleasures of being beside both sea and river the idea had a frosty reception. So Barmouth it was. We had a splendid day there and returned full of laughter and happiness. All I needed to round off the day was for the proprietor to have had a blank. As we returned he beckoned me over, took me through to the back regions and pointed to eight large, fresh-run, glistening salmon on his slab. 'Pity you couldn't come,' he said, 'the biggest run I've seen in the Mawddach and I had all these in the morning and lost a few others. Marvellous sport.' Ah well, you can't win them all, but Maureen thought I was a bit quiet and thoughtful over dinner. Perhaps I could handle it better now. After all, there were pictures of Prince Charles fishing on *his* honeymoon. And perhaps I could have persuaded Maureen that anything the Prince of Wales does ought to be good enough example for us.

The Usk has pleasant memories for me with those two early salmon and many other entertaining hours of trout fishing, but it has no sizable run of sea-trout and the salmon fishing is inconsistent. The Wye has few sea-trout, but it deserves its reputation as the outstanding salmon river in Wales. It was on the Wye that Pashley had his fabulous catches, often taking several hundred salmon in a season. In his later years much of his fishing was from a boat, but when he was catching so many from the bank his interesting technique for landing them was to choose a spot with shelving sand or mud bottom and stir it up so that the water was clouded. That is also a method favoured by that modern authority on salmon fishing, Arthur Oglesby.

Pashley took 535 salmon in one season, mainly on fly. In 1912 he killed 101 salmon in just twenty-two days' fishing, and in 1926 once had fifteen, once sixteen fish in a day all on fly. But if Pashley was the most renowned of Wye fishermen, the best of the writers on the river was H. A. Gilbert, whose *Tale of a Wye Fisherman* is a classic. 'Barmy' Gilbert was also an outstanding cricketer, who took 8 for 71 against Noble's Australians when playing for Oxford University with Tony Pawson's father in 1909. His nickname may well have come from a fishing addiction so extreme that on one occasion he went straight from a wedding reception to fish in topper and tails, and was soon wading in to fight a fish with scant regard for his morning dress. Not surprisingly, he was a broad-minded and intelligent performer in a sport which is often bedevilled by narrow-minded prejudice. This, for instance, is a telling passage from the 1953 edition of his book: 'When I was very young I lived far up the Wye where no one used any lure but the sacred fly. The mention of any kind of bait was anathema to all of us. We were all so "pure" that we gave no consideration whatever to unlucky mortals who fished far away in waters very different in character from our own. I was "purist" once myself, but soon fell from grace. The Tempter was an aged visitor who came to us one arid August, and with a wicked grin produced an odoriferous bottle of prawns. Very soon a fish attached itself to one of these "whiskered stinka-dores" and shot madly down the rapids below, pursued by an aged sinner, old enough to have known better, and an excited small boy yelling and brandishing a gaff. Many purists are produced on the upper Wye because in fact they cannot use a spinning reel, and can't master the subtle art of the minnow. I have heard one say he hated minnow fishing because his line always tangled up!'

Gilbert indicated that the reliance on flyfishing was in the favoured reaches from Boughrood upstream and that by the 1950s 'Wye methods in general are certainly, on two-thirds of the river, concerned with bait chiefly, in early spring, and that bait is almost entirely minnow.' He added that this type of fishing had been revolutionised once H. C. Hatton evolved a light minnow sliding easily up the trace, to replace the heavy Devon Minnow, which had so often caught on the bottom.

Using a Nottingham reel and the light aluminium minnows, Hatton developed the very successful Wye style of fishing as described by Gilbert: 'The proper way of fishing such a minnow is not to reel in the bait at all, but to throw the minnow slightly downstream, using only sufficient lead to keep the light bait down and to allow the minnow to drift round and across the pool exactly like a fly. The lightness of the bait gives life to the lure and as it crosses the stream it sways and swings with every tiny alteration and eddy of the current, whereas the heavy minnow ploughs its way across, stolid and unappetising. Moreover the heavy minnow usually spins sitting up on its tail, a very unnatural attitude for a minnow, and not horizontally as a light minnow does.'

Gilbert's advice holds good today and is the basis of much of my fishing with Mepps rather than Devons. It is interesting to see the emphasis he also puts on 'presentation', on making the bait 'appetising'. There indeed is the secret of all successful fishing. He is also right to underline the skills of minnow fishing as in this further passage: 'In my view long throwing of the minnow is one of the great arts and one of the most delightful "minor tactics" of minnow fishing. Only a good judge of distance and direction can score by these means and it is a delight to pick up a fish under the opposite bank after arduous efforts.'

He was however primarily a flyfisherman, like me, and confirmed the excellence of the Wye in this regard. He and Pashley caught the majority of their salmon on fly when the water was well-suited to this method or was in what Gilbert regarded as perfect condition for fly: 'That is, firstly, when the temperature of the water has been low for long periods; secondly, there is a large run of fish; thirdly there have been many small rises in the height of the water, and fourthly, when the Lugg and Ithon mud does not foul the river.'

Those 'big runs' are not so common now, nor the Wye so teeming with parr as it used to be. That is odd when the netting stations have been progressively bought out and such care is lavished on the river. But at least it remains a fine salmon river with its prospect of 'portmanteau' fish.

The Wye is noted for its great 'portmanteau' fish, which run as big as any in Britain. In the past several salmon have been taken in the Wye within a pound or two of that record fish of 64 lbs taken by the slim, small Georgina Ballantyne on the Tay in 1922. Her great salmon, hooked at dusk on a revolving brown lure called a 'dace', was gaffed two hours later by her boatman father and was only some eight inches shorter than Georgina herself. The Wye hasn't produced anything quite as big, though some sixty-pounders have been taken from it in years gone by. But it has rarely been a lucky river for me. I have fished its broad stretch at Wyesham below Monmouth. Always I seem to be there the week before or the week after the salmon were running and taking. How many chapters of a salmon fisher's life story that experience covers!

The one minor triumph I had on it was far upriver, near Erwood. The beat was just below the Nith water, with its deep spectacular channels, where the Ashley Coopers have taken so many fish. The water was high and coloured and when I hooked a fish I soon saw the gleam of it in the water. 'Just a small one,' I said to myself. But it's often difficult to judge the weight of a salmon on your line unless it jumps. So many times the eye is deceived by the refraction in the water or by a glimpse of its length without seeing how broad is the back, how round the belly. When the net slid under this one it was not as easy to lift as I had expected. To my delight the salmon was a typical stocky Wye fish, short but so solid that I was left celebrating my first twenty-pounder. I had fished for twenty years before catching one of the size which had for so long been a target in my mind. That Wye fish so changed my luck that I had two more even larger before the end of the season, one of 21½ lbs from Abercothi and a 26 lb fish from the Tweed.

The Tweed at Kelso for me provides the most exciting of Scottish salmon fishing. It is one of Scotland's largest rivers and already broad and deep as it flows on towards Berwick. The Kelso water includes the Junction Beat, where the Teviot runs in, and a fine Bridge Pool below. Lower down is another favourite of mine, Sprouston, which divides into The Bushes and The Dub, a reach almost quarter of a mile long. Junction Beat caters for six rods, with three usually fishing from the bank and three from the boats needed to cover such wide water properly; Sprouston takes two rods, both from boats. The Tweed has a well-deserved reputation for its huge autumn runs of salmon and I have been lucky enough to be invited there when the November fishing is at its best. My most recent visit was the best of all, with the water full of fish and a thirty-pounder taken on the beat the day I arrived. After a good start I lost a heavy fish myself. It took me down to the backing, which rarely happens to me, so I hadn't bothered to check it for some time. I paid for the error when it parted under the strain and thirty yards of line was gone for good with it.

Two days later at the Bridge Pool I hooked a fish which played deep and pulled hard but in the water it showed reddish and looked small, so I wasn't too concerned about landing it. So heavy was the strain exerted on it that I was surprised it took over ten minutes to net. Billy was my gillie for the day and as he lifted out the net he gave a whoop of pleasure. 'Look at the size of it! Ye'll no catch many larger.' Certainly I'd never caught a larger one before. It weighed 27½ lbs. Then I saw Billy laughing. He'd just tested the cast and the twenty-pound nylon had parted as if it was thin thread. Why it had held while I played that fish so hard seemed to have no rational explanation. But then salmon fishing so often defies logic – that's a part of its continuing fascination.

Directly above the Junction Beat are the Upper and Lower

Floors, two fine beats on the Duke of Roxburgh's fishing. This same season Arthur Oglesby caught there the largest salmon he had taken in British waters. It weighed 27½ lbs. It's nice to be running level with so fine a fisherman, but I was amused that he caught it while making a part of the remarkable Benson & Hedges Flyfishing Video (which runs for two hours and has a wealth of fine photography and good advice). For my own experience has also been that the salmon seem ready to star in films and hook on more easily when the cameras are on them! At least the video records just what it's like to play a large salmon on this lovely river. The Tay is another Scottish river with a great reputation, which appears well-deserved from my only experience of it. Fishing at Stanley near Perth I quickly had two fine salmon of around 19 lbs each, before a flood ended what might have been some memorable fishing. On this river, noted for big fish, the most unusual I saw was a tiddler by comparison. It was a small sea-trout and round its middle was a rubber band, which had scarred it and still cut deeply into it. It must have swum through the band or had it put over, then been progressively squeezed as it grew and the band contracted. It was said that boys sometimes put such bands on parr before returning them to the water. It might seem harmless fun at the time, but it was no fun at all to see how later the fish had been wounded and distorted by the band.

The Tweed is a joy to fish at any time, but in early spring there's a very different run of fish. The salmon then are mostly below ten pounds – bright, lively springers full of fight, but far from heavyweights. With the water cold and high, spinner will normally outscore fly, and for me one year came a striking demonstration of this. In the first two weeks of February only fly is permitted. The day before the spinning season started the water appeared almost empty of fish, only one falling to six rods and their large, hard-worked flies. But next day more than twenty were taken in these pools as the Golden Sprats and Devon Minnows searched them out. As the water warms and drops fly again comes into its own. But whatever the month, whatever the method, this great river is a salmon fisherman's delight.

7

Fishing Friends and Characters

You can fish in isolation and still be totally absorbed in the sport but for me a main part of its attraction is the friendly contacts you make and the companionable association with like-minded anglers. One all-round fisherman with whom I have had a long and happy acquaintance is Terry Thomas. Terry has done a lot to give the sport favourable publicity, to help disabled anglers, and to promote proper fishing instruction. He is also very knowledgeable on fishing tackle and has given me much useful advice both on that and on fishing methods. Terry has involved me in making fishing films for television, and highly entertaining some of that has been. The advantage of such films being produced under the guidance of a true angler is that they concentrate on fishing naturally, without the sort of gimmicks often introduced in the belief that fishing has to be 'jazzed up' to be a presentable television spectacle, a peculiar but widely held belief among producers who are not themselves fishermen. But Terry will only involve himself with showing the sport as it really is, knowing well the magnetic attraction it has for so many.

Yet you can never be quite natural before television cameras. With the large crews, the problems of siting the cameras, the plethora of equipment, and the pressure to catch fish rapidly, it is inevitably an unnatural situation, with unnatural tension. But the salmon do act naturally before the cameras – at least in the sense of retaining their infinite capacity to astonish the angler. The most remarkable salmon I've ever caught was in a filming session on the Teifi, on the Llandyssul Water. The pool had been fished down several times by a visiting angler and Artie Jones had also done his best to conjure up a fish. Then the camera crew milled around, splashing into the water, noisily planting equipment along the bank and scaring any sensible fish within miles. Finally the producer turned to me and said: 'I want you to catch a salmon quickly, Gareth, as the light's just right.' With brilliant sunshine adding to the impossibility of taking a fish in the low, clear water, I told him he must be joking. 'All I can do is to cast to the best of my ability. But if you must have a shot of playing a salmon you'll have to use your ingenuity; get someone to pull the end of the line and focus only on me and a bending rod, or my running reel, then mix in some shots of a leaping salmon from other footage; or do something else clever and contrived. But don't expect *me* to hook one.'

I was pleased enough with the precision of my first cast – but left witless as a salmon cruised up from the bottom and seized the fly. I was almost paralysed with shock, so unexpected was it. After my strident briefing the television crew were focused on me and missed the take. So thoroughly had I convinced them no fish was possible I was afraid it might come off before they realised there really was a salmon to film. A lively fight it was, too, with the camera crew contentedly recording the playing and capture of a 10 lb fish. When it took I had been startled into striking it as if it were a trout, without letting go of the loop of line in my hand. So I had hooked it lightly in the lip and was fortunate indeed to land it. One of my own rugby idols, Dewi Bebb, was presenter of this HTV film, and not being a fisherman himself he accepted it as the most natural thing for me to have done and only what he expected of a fellow Welsh Rugby International!

Whenever Terry Thomas and I went filming on salmon rivers I was usually on form and fortunate in my catches. Perhaps the tension made one fish harder and better; I don't really believe the fish were as eager to get themselves on the screen as most humans. Once on the Junction Beat of the

Tweed at Kelso I caught four fine fish in a morning's filming. And there was a day there in November when I seemed able to catch to order, as Terry had me filming again on the Hawthorns Pool on Junction Beat. The sky was clear, the sun low, the light soft – a marvellous morning for the cameras if only I could catch fish, as Terry assured me I would. Catch them I did, in rapid succession. After I had landed a couple I found I was meant to play them to order as well as hooking them when required. As I struggled with a salmon the cameraman issued a stream of instructions. 'Back up a bit, it'll make a much better shot. Bring him down now. I want him landed right under the camera.' Then I was into a 16 lb fish, concentrating solely on his fierce rushes. The orders began again. 'Move down the bank towards us. Now stand under that tree – why can't you do what we ask?' He was under the impression that I was controlling the fish, whereas a salmon that size was controlling me. But by the end of three concentrated days I had thirteen salmon, the largest 19 lbs, and everyone was happy. Terry has an infectious humour, chuckling away as he watches you fish. Wise and experienced, he has always helped to put me in the mood to catch fish. Confidence is ninety per cent of the secret of fishing and Terry had transmitted some of his own to me.

Jim Miller is another fishing companion to whom I owe many enlivening days on the Tweed. Jim is chairman of the Harris and Sheldon Group which owns Hardys, the prestigious firm whose fishing tackle I find lives up to its high reputation. He has often invited me to join him on that beat at Kelso where the Teviot joins the Tweed, indeed that was where he had permitted the filming with Terry Thomas; and on such a productive beat you always fish with keen expectation. There is, too, the inevitable friendly rivalry between members of the party including Jim's wife Flo. She is as competitive as she is capable, and delights in catching more than several eminent anglers manage who fish the beat.

In 1981 I was invited up for three days and arrived full of eager anticipation only to find the river high and some of the rods leaving because the fishing was poor. In unpromising conditions I caught two good fish on the first day, both giving me a hard fight in the high water. Next day the river was fining down, the conditions perfect, the fish there in plenty – and I had a blank, without even a touch. That's frustrating enough when you know you ought to be catching them, but now there were jokes to endure as well from more successful anglers. I tried to keep my confidence and my end up with the other rods by asserting that I was bound to do well on the morrow: 'It's Saturday and I'm always at my best then – particularly at 3 pm' I just had to hope that the salmon too were lively at kick-off time!

Unfortunately next morning they didn't seem to be lively at all. I was fishing The Dub on Sprouston, that long stretch with a strong flow throughout and a weir at the bottom. I started full of expectancy at 9.30 in the morning, but hope dulled when I had again moved nothing after two hours. Then came a heavy pull as my golden sprat searched the current. It was clearly a big fish, and on the Tweed that sets the pulses racing: you never know *how* big. Then came that heartbreak moment as the rod sprang straight and I was left wondering if I'd just lost the fish of a lifetime. Only those who have experienced it know the bitter disappointment of such moments and in my depression I imagined the whole day was to be one of disaster. But the fish were moving now and in quick succession I had four fresh, silvery salmon as a great run came into the pool. The blank was forgotten and even the large fish lost was barely an ache in the memory. The heavy weight of fish was no burden on the walk back, and after the previous leg-pulling I wasn't too upset to find that Jim had nothing to show for his morning's fishing on the Bushes Pool above. For the short afternoon session we switched, with Jim going to The Dub, myself to The Bushes. And the fish did indeed kick off for me about 3 pm and stayed so active that I had five more. They were all silvery-looking and played like springers except the fifth. The gillie had encouraged me not to reel in at the day's end, saying: 'Go on. Have one more throw.' Happily I did, for there was another strong

pull, another large fish hooked. The battle lasted twenty minutes, with the salmon making runs of eighty yards or so before
it tired, then boring down into deep water. It was a big back-
ender weighing 26½ lbs, in beautiful condition and looking
wonderful to me, even if it was rather red. That was a fine
climax to my best day's salmon fishing, and one on which six
rods caught twenty-four between them.

Fishing the broad Scottish rivers is an experience which is
greatly enhanced by the gillies who look after you so well.
Each, of course, has his own characteristics and personality
but in my experience they have several things in common. The
first is a great love of the outdoors and a willingness to pass on
their own accumulated fishing knowledge to those sensible
enough to ask. I am always eager to seek their advice, for no
one knows their own waters, or the moods of the fish, as well
as they do. Even more important is the truth that they are keen
to share an angler's experience rather than the traditional
myth that all they want to share is his dram of whisky. They are
as excited as you when you catch a fish and suffer with you the
agony of a large one lost.

There is a nice passage about gillies in *The Haig Guide to
Salmon Fishing in Scotland*: 'A gillie is half sportsman, half
entertainer, but for those new to gilliedom there are one or two
dos and don'ts. Never call him by his surname only – unless
your own name appears in Debrett. Let him put up your rod if
he likes – but never let him fish for you. Treat him as the wise
and entertaining person he certainly is – and he will add stars
to your holiday. Times have even brought changes to the
unchanging gillies. You are unlikely to meet anyone like the
famous Leekie, who ruled over some fishing on Deeside 40
years ago. Beautifully mannered, immensely knowledgeable,
he would arrive each morning in immaculately cut tweed
plus-fours, shoes burnished, handle-brush moustache oiled
and gleaming. Yet when his fisherman hooked a salmon he
would not hesitate to stride into the river, fully clothed, to net
it.'

When I go to the Tweed or the Dee it is in the anticipated

pleasure of seeing old friends again among the gillies. Unless my performance is up to the mark, there will be comments such as 'I hope your rugby is better than your fishing!' But when I do catch, it changes to: 'Wales 3, Scotland 0'. And each will have his special favourite among the various flies or lures. On the Tweed Bert may ponder other items in his box but the advice will always be to use a Golden Sprat. And its small trebles certainly hook fish well. But Gordon will advise a Yellow Belly Minnow and for flyfishing will naturally recommend a Gordon's Fancy with yellow hackle and black body.

On the wide boat pools of the Tweed you are very dependent on the gillie to put you in the right place at the right angle to fish. It's their skill with the boat which influences your catch as much as your casting, and they have to remain cheerful and attentive even when dodging the miscasts of poor anglers. As Norman put it to me: 'I'm glad when some anglers leave and I can take the bucket off my head!' That was only half in jest — he'd had a treble in his retina on one occasion.

There's no danger of that with another with whom I fish there, Jim Hardy. The perfection of his casting is an education in itself and is usually rewarded with good catches. Also fishing there has been another of those expert all-rounders I so admire. Fred Buller is best known for his definitive writing on pike fishing, but he seemed just as knowledgeable and effective in pursuit of salmon, and he kept us entertained with accounts of fishing on Mask, his favourite Irish lough. Like Lough Erne in Northern Ireland Mask has monster brown trout as well as huge pike. When a big trout takes the fly in that rocky, limestone lough there is what the locals call a 'brown wink', as you glimpse the mouth opening and closing.

In the past most of the large trout on Mask were taken on trolled spoons but a number are also taken on wet fly and Fred talked of the feats of local hero, Robby O'Grady, who has caught more than fifty double-figure trout in the lough. The favoured wet flies are the traditional Irish Green or Brown Peters, various coloured Murraghs and the more common stillwater patterns like the Soldier Palmer, or Black Pennel.

Almost as much pleasure comes from the scenery as from the fish you
catch: this is the Lower Kaitum Lake.

The tensions of sea-fishing off Gothenburg are stretched tighter in front of the television cameras during the Fishing Race in Sweden.

After some good battles I manage to land grayling from a Lapland river during the Fishing Race.

The beautiful Waitahanui River in New Zealand flows into Taupo Lake; both provide marvellous fishing.

My host on Waitahanui, Graham Thorne, a former All Black centre.

From late May, for the period of the rise, the Mayfly can also be deadly. One of the delights described by Fred was dapping with Mayfly or Daddy Longlegs and seeing big trout take them with a swirl or a leap. Mayfly time, when so many trout congregate in the shallows, is when many monster trout come in from deep water to feed on the 'bite-sized' fish and that's when most of them are caught. As a brown trout of 17½ lbs, only a pound below the British record, was recently caught in Mask, I'm sure the lough will continue to draw Fred in the hopes of one even larger. I hope the Tweed continues to draw him too, for he is as good a communicator as angler, a wise and witty man who can discourse about port or claret as fluently as about catching salmon or pike. In meeting such people your imagination is stirred by realising how much more they know about fishing, how much more there is for you to experience. The more you talk, the more you discover of unexplored opportunity or challenge.

George Heaney, a former chairman and managing director of General Motors in Scotland, is another fishing enthusiast to whom I have reason to be grateful. It was he who first introduced me to the Royal Dee in the stretch below Banchory. On my first visit there he took me down on the late afternoon of my arrival to walk the beat. Never have I seen so many salmon showing. Every five seconds, it seemed, one swirled or jumped; the river appeared to be teeming with fish. I didn't dream of catching them that night because I never even got to sleep. So powerful was the impact on my mind that I couldn't wait for the morning to come as I restlessly pictured the great fish I would catch. In fact the salmon were in teasing mood and reality didn't quite live up to expectation. But the picture of so many fish moving in this lovely river had already made an indelible impression on my mind. When they decide to take you can have a remarkable day there, as with a novice lady who took six in a morning. Even if I've never done as well, the Dee is bracketed in my mind with the Tweed for perfection of Scottish salmon fishing.

The other debt I owe George is for giving me the chance to

spend time with one of my sporting heroes, Jack Nicklaus. For me he is the world's greatest competitor and a real gentleman of sport, never sparing himself and always helpful to others. George got to know him well on his business trips to America, and in view of Jack's passion for fishing was always ready to offer him a rod on the Dee if he could spare time from his golf. 1983 became memorable for me with my love of that game because, all within a few weeks, I had formed a winning partnership with Hugh Baiocchi in a competition at San Pierre, then played in a BBC televised event with Tom Watson and, to climax it all, had taken part in the same golfing occasion as Jack Nicklaus. George Heaney, chairman also of the Glasgow Chamber of Commerce, had persuaded Jack to come over for the 200th anniversary celebrations and to play a few holes with a variety of sporting personalities. Not only did George invite me to be one of the golfers, but asked that I fly up with Jack.

Nicklaus had flown overnight from Miami and was understandably tired as the private aircraft took us on from Heathrow to Glasgow. For him, no doubt, it was misfortune that strong headwinds slowed the flight far behind schedule when all he can have wanted was to get there and get to bed. But for me it was a wonderful chance to talk fishing with a man who has the same passion for it as I have and who has had the chance to fish in so many parts of the world.

Tired as Jack was the light was back in his eye as soon as we talked about fishing – it was clear that he was just as dedicated and competent in this sport too. As I had found, fishing was for him the ideal foil to the pressures of his own game. Whenever his punishing schedule allowed, he was able to lose himself in its timeless world, the absorption, the peace of mind and the relaxation refreshing him for his next contest. Much of his fishing has been for the great monsters of the sea: out with Kerry Packer off the coast of Australia he had an epic battle with a blue marlin which was close to record size. From his Florida home he can go off and fish the Florida Flats, catching a variety of sea fish and those bone fish which in shallow water are the most spectacular fighters of any. When I asked him what type of fishing gave him most pleasure, though, he hesitated only a moment over the two possible choices in his mind. His final preference was for Atlantic salmon, with the excitement of tarpon fishing coming a close second.

Jack's favourite salmon fishing method is one too little practised over here. Mostly he fishes for them with bushy dry flies, which he finds catch him as many and give him a greater thrill in the catching. The take is for most fishermen the supreme moment of the sport. With the dry fly you see the great shape of the salmon come gliding up to the surface and need to control your nerves not to strike too soon. On the evidence of his golf, Jack can never have any difficulty controlling *his* iron nerve. In traditional fishing areas, his preference for the dry fly brings polite smiles. Iceland is one of his favourites for salmon fishing, and large catches are the rule rather than the exception there. But on one river he arrived to find that not many had been caught in the previous few days. When he started with his dry flies the locals laughed outright and advised him not to waste his time. Within a couple of hours he had the satisfaction of three good fish on the bank and the laughter now changed to earnest enquiry.

There is no surprise for me that top performers in a number of sports find equal pleasure in their fishing. As Jack rightly commented, it provides the ideal contrast to the demands of their public appearances and the pressure at top-level competition. At the same time it satisfies their competitive natures, but in a quieter way. Soccer's Jack Charlton is typical of a man who is just as happy on the riverbank, whether fishing for salmon or pike, as he was when helping to win the World Cup at Wembley. Ian Botham is most people's idea of the all-action man, a non-stop powerhouse of energy, but he too is a devotee of the 'contemplative' sport.

Sportsmen or entertainers who catch the public imagination have many demands on them. There is the physical and mental effort devoted to performing consistently well in top-level competition, and also the pressure of being forever in the spotlight of public comment and criticism. So often this is overgenerous when all is going well and they have no need of kindness but callously brutal when what they need is reassurance and support. There are many compensations for them, but little peace of mind. The Beatles needed a guru to help them find it; Bob Willis has his hypnotic tapes to aid his relaxation before major matches; Billy Connolly, if you take a humorous advertisement seriously, relies on Heineken to refresh his parts. Not so Ian Botham. For him, as for many other sportsmen, like Jack Nicklaus and myself, fishing is the perfect foil, the saving tranquillity. As Ian put it to me: 'I have no need of a guru or any artificial aids so long as I have time to fish. This is the ideal relaxation, away from all the pressures of everyday life. I am at peace on lake or river, totally absorbed in the pursuit of game fish, the sight and sound of running water, the beauty of the scenery in Scotland or Somerset.'

Ian is now a dedicated angler and the sport is a vital part of his life. He was, however, no instant convert. Early on he did some coarse fishing without enjoying it much. Not until he was eighteen did he experience the fascination of game fishing, with salmon soon becoming a prime target, a prime interest. As in my case his first salmon was a long time landing – eight years in fact. With Ian, too, the more prolonged the chase, the more desirable the prize became. What had begun to appear an impossible dream was realised at last on a favourite river of his, the Teith, near Callander. Ian was spinning with a green and gold Toby when the salmon took. It was a small one, just 6 lbs, but for Ian it was matchless in form and taste. So the Teith draws him back year after year; he has fished there for ten or more. Ian is another who knows there's much more to fishing than catching fish – the place and the people are equally important. He finds the refreshment of spirit he needs seeking salmon or sea-trout on the Teith, or trout fishing on a private lake in Somerset. As he says: 'The other great joy of fishing is in the marvellous friends you meet and the completely relaxed atmosphere in which you can enjoy the friendships. It is this which makes the sport so pleasant and so important to me.'

Even when salmon fishing Ian can't entirely evade publicity. He fishes often with Stan Piecha, the angling correspondent of *The Sun*. But that, too, is a firm friendship, for Stan is entertaining company as I found myself when fishing with him in a television programme in Ireland. How does 'Both' the sportsman-angler rate the writer? 'Stan is an outstanding coarse angler, but still a bit of a novice with salmon. He may stay that way for a season or two yet, because he is your typical angling writer – for every half-hour he's fishing he spends two hours chatting. That's why he is such a good journalist!'

Ian Botham himself is a typical all-rounder in any sport he attempts. He has to be in the action all the time. So he is becoming expert at taking salmon on fly, spinner, prawn, or worm (or the Blackbirds' Fancy, as some Scots call it trying to kid you they are flyfishing). All game fish fascinate him and he has made himself just as competent catching trout on small stillwaters. Like many sportsmen he finds angling satisfies both the need to relax and the innate desire to excel. For someone as competitive as Ian, it's a change not to *have* to compete, but inevitably he conforms to Walton's description of the true angler as one who has an ambition to be among the best in his art.

Jack Nicklaus's enjoyment of fishing in Iceland has been shared by Tony Pawson, as he recorded for me: 'Icelandic salmon fishing has always been outstanding and is likely to remain so because of their sensible management of their rivers. They appreciated that anglers made the best use of their migratory fish resource, bringing in most money and culling only a small proportion of the stock since fishing is so in-efficient compared to netting. As angling was much more valuable to the country, involved more people, and helped keep the right balance of fish in the river the Icelandics have excluded any netting in the rivers and manage them solely for the benefit of the fish and the angler. But it was not because of this that I first went to fish there. My family doctor, the late Geoffrey Harrison, was also a great ornithologist and spent a lot of time in Iceland studying harlequin ducks, the only ones to live in the fast water of rivers. He arranged with the head of Iceland Air in London for me to fish in the north of the island. The planned itinerary was to fly to Reykjavik, then on to the northern capital of Akureyri and on by bus to Husavik and the great Laxa River flowing to the sea there. The first leg went fine and we flew into Reykjavik over the spectacular eruptions of Sertse, creating a new lava island in the sea. At the airport two Iceland Air pilots sought me out, saying they had been asked to accompany me on the fishing trip and that a friend of theirs would fly us to Husavik and so cut out the bus journey. What they didn't say was that this involved flying round all the little airfields on the coast. For an inexperienced air traveller there were nervous moments, landing on fields which were no more than a strip of lava with a wind-sock flying in the corner. So when we touched down at Husavik I hurried towards the back of the plane and was far from overjoyed to be told to sit down again as their pilot friend proposed to land on the road near the fishing hut. The 'road' was a wide expanse of black lava-like surface and seemed happily devoid of traffic as we finally put down safely enough.

'The next problem was the fishing hut. Two other friends joined my airline companions there and in its tiny confines there was hardly room for us all to sleep and cook for the week of the fishing. Moreover, the stock of food was dried fish, dried horsemeat, and more dried fish and horsemeat, all of which I found totally inedible. So for the week I was there I was fishing for existence, living on the sea-trout I caught and the berries, looking and tasting similar to blueberries, which I picked off the bushes outside.

'Fortunately the sea-trout were plentiful and eager to take the fly. But, particularly with salmon, the river presented an unusual problem. "You won't mind a few floating weeds, will you?" they had said to me in London when booking the beat. Confident that my casting ability would avoid any such minor obstruction I had indicated that I could take them in my stride. But it wasn't a few weeds. Higher up, the river flowed through lakes that were a sea of weed from which trailing tendrils were continually swept away, so the whole river below was a moving mass of tiny weed fragments. No sooner had you shot your line to full length than the weed began to attach itself to the fly. And as you pulled in the line to clear it, the weed built up on the line trailing in the water. So after every few casts you had to reel in, cleaning the line as you did so and then the fly before casting it out again. Worse, when a fish was hooked the weed began to collect round the join of cast and line, rapidly growing to the size of a football. The rod was bent double just playing the weed, with virtually no pressure on the salmon. So the first five I hooked all came off long before I could solve the problem.

'My companions were all worm fishermen who could give me no useful advice. But there was a great feeling of exhilaration when at last I landed one, and a large one at that. The heavy fish played so long that the weed built to unusual size, until I thought we had reached perpetual stalemate. The fish had tired, but it was all the rod could do to lift the great mass of weed above the surface while the salmon wiggled quietly a cast's length away from me. It was nearly an hour before I managed to edge out beside it, going well over my trouser waders, and grip its tail. That woke it up again and there was a wild and exhausting struggle before a 19 lb fish and I lay on the bank, both equally exhausted. Only when the week was nearly up did I find a pool where the current appeared to clean the weed away. There the fishing was fabulous, the takes as frequent as if fishing for sea-trout rather than salmon.

'There followed a strange solitary week dedicated to trout fishing on the upper Laxa, where the water ran clear above the weeded lakes. My farmhouse "digs" were in high bleak hill country beautified for me only by the river at the door. This was a tumble of white water broadening into swirling pools before racing on over the next rapid. The river ran bright and sparkling over its rocky bed, the banks were grassy, the fishing easy.

'My bedroom was clean and comfortable, the morning and evening meals mountainous and wholesome. My hosts and I understood not a word of the other's language and communicated with smiles and nods and pointing fingers. Trying to find where to fish I waved my rod and spread wide my arms in dumb enquiry. They pointed me vaguely in the direction of some downstream pools and the first afternoon was wasted before I found it was only a side-stream I was fishing. Next morning I crossed the rickety footbridge and hit the main river at an ideal spot. There a swift shallow run-in spread out round and wide, forming a small lake rather than just a pool. The bottom here was muddy but firm, the depth uniform over its whole expanse. Everywhere the water came near the top of my trouser waders but never over them, though in places I was fishing a-tiptoe. There were plenty of trout in the run-in, plenty on the edge of the fast current sweeping over to the far bank, plenty in the quiet at the tail.

'There were no other houses in sight, but from a village beyond the crest occasional anglers came down the opposite bank. They fished with spinners in the fast run without apparent success. Yet for me the flyfishing was the best I have ever had for wild brown trout. They took eagerly the size 8 Black Pennel on the tail, but even more eagerly the Blue Pennel dropper bobbed across the current, or on the rippled tail where the wind ruffled the surface. In this country of fire and freeze with its hot springs, its geysers, its molten lava so close below the cold crust of earth, I fished on enthralled as an August snowstorm swirled around me. That wintry hour brought frenzied activity in this remarkable pool with the larger fish coming to feed.

'Each day I spent a couple of hours exploring this intriguing river for half a mile on either side. Yet the many other inviting runs yielded only one trout, while sixty-seven came in just five days from that one special pool. The trout were plump and well-conditioned though I saw no sign of any abundant fly life or natural rises. They ranged from ¾ lb upwards. Eighteen of those I caught were 3 lbs or over, with three of them up to 5 lbs and one of 6¼ lbs, a spectacular fish which gave a spectacular fight.

'Each morning my breakfast was left ready for me and I was off early to the river. In the evening the bag of trout was handed over to be smoked or salted down for the winter. They accepted the fish with smiles of gratitude and the dinner was then silently served. Only as I packed for the long bus ride back to Husavik was the monastic routine broken. A small deputation arrived from the village with one spokesman capable of a few words of English: "Would you be pleased to leave one of the magic flies?" he asked. So I parted with my last two Blue Pennels, and perhaps imitation patterns are catching big trout there yet. The flies were size 8 well hackled, but old and faded in colour so that they seemed more a mixture of black and grey than blue. But I kept no sample myself of the fly on which some fifty of those trout were taken. And never since have I been able to match those Blue Pennels exactly, nor come near to matching such remarkable fishing for wild brown trout.'

It has been my good fortune always to have expert local advice on my Welsh rivers from the likes of Artie Jones, Bryn Evans, Graham Evans and Ken Edwards. I have always sought it, welcomed it, and tested it against my own experience and experiments. That is the best way to improve and get even greater enjoyment from your sport. Particularly is it helpful in getting to know where to fish at different heights of water, or times of day, or seasons of the year. On method and baits and flies there are so many theories that you can confuse yourself. I tend to agree with some words of wisdom passed on to me by Ken Edwards. He had just given some good advice that I should go up or down a size in flies to catch a fish which had moved but not taken before. Then he added: 'I've tried everything in my time. But in fishing it's a case of the simpler, the better. If you find where and when they are taking you'll catch them with anything, *if* you present it right. And if they aren't in the mood nothing is going to tempt them.' But then Ken always seems to know where they are taking and presents his size 4 Mepps to their satisfaction.

Apart from my fishing friends I feel an affinity for a man I've never met but who took my own fishing experience to extremes. Like me, Hugh Clement was a Sawdde trout fisherman until salmon and sea-trout changed the pattern of his life. As he recorded in *The Salmon & Trout Magazine*, his fishing career really started when a salmon leapt over his little trout fly. Surely capturing one could not be all that difficult? As his wife pointed out, they had much bigger mouths than trout, with a larger area to hook! So he deserted the Sawdde for a fishing syndicate on the Cothi. The quest was hard and long. As he put it: 'After three years I realised Salmon were unpredictable. After five years I realised Salmon were not very easy to catch. After eight years I gave up Salmon fishing and went after sea-trout. As my wife pointed out, their mouths were smaller so they might be easier to hook.'

Salmon stayed in his mind as the only fish deserving a capital letter, but the sea-trout proved difficult too: 'After two years I realised they were wary. After three years I realised they were elusive. After five years I caught one!' As often happens, that first capture brought renewed confidence and a winter study of Hugh Falkus's *Sea-Trout Fishing* improved method to the point where the following season he had some thirty sea-trout up to 7 lbs. On a favourite pool he also developed an unusual but useful marker: on the far bank was a colony of glow worms, which helped him keep direction with his night casting. One October evening while wetting his line at 7.15 pm in the run-in to the pool, his Esmond Drury No 6, with its silver body, red tag and black squirrel hair-wing, was seized by a massive fish. After an hour and twenty minutes of struggle in the dark his torch revealed a 14 lb salmon in the net. 'Not possible,' said his angling friends. But it *was* a salmon he had landed at last and, as he commented happily: 'It took me seventeen years to do it.'

The impact of that fish will have been all the greater for the long wait, the unexpected capture. Hugh Clement clearly has the qualities a salmon fisher needs – perseverance and patience. His moment of triumph will live with him all his life, and with one the net plenty of others will follow. Clearly he'll relish every one just as I do.

8

Stillwater Trout Fishing

Salmon and sea-trout rivers are the happy hunting ground of my fishing, but the joy of catching trout has never left me, so I can still take pleasure in the occasional day on a stocked stillwater. I can well appreciate, too, how the development of these waters has brought flyfishing and trout fishing within the reach of nearly a million anglers who might otherwise miss the enjoyment of the sport. For me, though, this type of fishing is not the peak of attraction – the playing of fish is so much easier than in streams, and rainbow trout are the main quarry rather than the more graceful and colourful browns. But it can be entertaining enough, especially when fishing such waters with an expert in the methods involved: in any sport there is a special fascination in watching a topclass performer. That is certainly true of fishing, with so many skills and techniques involved, so much to learn or appreciate. As far as stillwaters are concerned those techniques are somewhat different on the small lake from those on the large reservoir, so I found it intensely interesting when Tony Pawson and I fished each type with an acknowledged authority with whom to discuss the skills involved.

The visit to Chew Valley Lake provided also a memorable fishing experience which highlighted for me both the enjoyable and the frustrating elements of such fishing. The neighbouring Blagdon Lake was the prototype of these 'put and take' stillwaters and has remained supreme in reputation for the beauty of its setting and the quality of its trout. Chew is a larger, less intimate lake but it, too, fits naturally into the lovely Mendip landscape. The June day was as unpromising as could be, with a near-gale blowing and a bright sun glaring down from a cloudless sky. Fishing in those conditions was uncomfortable and fruitless, the lunch break suitably prolonged. At that time of the year at Chew and Blagdon there is always the hope of a good evening rise if conditions are calm enough and warm enough, and about six o'clock the wind did start to moderate just as Chris Ogborne came to join us. Chris is a marketing consultant for the Orvis tackle firm, a real expert on fishing these two lakes, with such a love of Blagdon that he has written a book about it. His technical ability is well attested by the fact that the first time he entered for the English National Flyfishing Championship he not only won through from the strong South-West Region, but won the Final as well, best of the sixty finalists at his first attempt. Chris is an extrovert character, full of good cheer, and his confidence that we would catch a lot of fish was just the reviver we needed. He had brought some other useful revivers as well, since he is also an area manager for Gonzalez Byass and well aware of the right moment for a refresher.

Chris took charge of the boat and pronounced the wind and conditions just right for a long drift from Denny Island over the False Island area and on to Nunnery Point. Apart from encouragement he also brought some specially tied flies and effective advice. There was still quite a ripple on the surface and no very heavy rise, but there were a few fish moving upwind and barely breaking the surface as they sipped in the buzzers. Being unused to this type of fishing I found it impossible at fist to spot them. Chris, however, had that second sight you develop with practice, seeming to sense every fish moving anywhere near us. He then directed my casting so that the flies entered the water a few yards in front and were working steadily by the time the trout reached them.

Earlier I had been using some standard Chew patterns, particularly the Grenadier and Soldier Palmer, which have such success there. Chris changed my tail fly to a small size 10

Muddler of his own tying, with black hackle and a bronze body. He said it would be deadly and it was. Soon I was regularly hooking fish and when Chris lent Tony one too it worked as well for him. The Chew rainbows were plump and supremely well-conditioned. They fought like wildcats too. 'Eat your heart out, Grafham and Rutland,' said Chris happily as the reel sang and I relished the fierce fights. 'No other reservoir produces trout like this!'

I could believe it as I savoured the pleasure of hooking and playing such splendid trout. There was indeed an enchantment about the evening, casting to seen fish and enjoying the thrill of the wild battles in several of which I came off second best. But though some escaped the net, I ended only one short of the limit of eight. What a contrast it was from the somewhat tedious chuck and chance of fishing during the day on a wide expanse of water neither of us knew too well, to the purposeful stalking of trout in the evening, with its rich rewards. At its best this type of fishing brings real excitement and satisfaction. At its worst I find it dull in comparison with the changes and challenges of a river: there, even when you can't move any fish, the next pool is always a new hope, a different test, a fresh scene. But that evening on Chew made me well aware how compelling lakes like Chew and Blagdon can be, how absorbed some fishermen can become in them.

In the carpark at Woodford Lodge at the start of the day I had been hailed by two golfing friends. They talked confidently of being experienced Chew anglers and offered to bet that they would catch a larger bag than us. It was a pity we declined, for as we walked back to the cars in the dark they were depressed, with only one fish between them, Tony and I elated with our dozen. The difference almost certainly lay in our having a local expert to guide us in the pattern of fly, the choice of location. The casual visitor will have his memorable days, but the locals who really get to know a water are the ones who will catch consistently.

Chris was particularly interesting about the flies, the tying of which appeared as much of a passion with him as the actual fishing on these two lovely lakes. 'Larger Muddlers often do

well on the dropper, but I was experimenting with size 10
Muddlers which can be fished in competitions limited to flies
of this hook size or smaller. And I've found that at this period
this pattern is proving deadly. But it is part of the fascination of
these two lakes that no one solution holds good for long. A few
seasons ago I had phenomenal success for some weeks with my
own version of a Green Nymph. Weighted or unweighted it
made limit bags standard for me. Then in the course of a few
days it ceased to take any fish at all, nor did any of the new
variants I hastily tied. Unless you keep adjusting your flies and
tactics as the water level changes, and the mood of the fish
changes, you are unlikely to catch consistently – unless you are
Steve Pope fishing Chew with a team of Grenadiers and always
seeming to bring home the fish!

'My father started me fishing at Chew and Blagdon just at
the time of the great post-war change from using large flies
worked fast on sunk lines as the normal method, to an
emphasis on nymphs and small flies on floaters. I was soon
attracted to using imitative patterns and the added pleasure of
making those patterns myself. The best present I ever received
from my father, the best present any youngster could get, was a
fly-tying vice and the basic essentials of a kit – scissors, hackle
pliers and bobbin holder. That in turn makes you study the fly
life and you soon realise why Black Buzzers or Grenadiers are
so attractive to the trout in the appropriate months. The old
advice was "Dark day, dark fly; bright day, bright fly," but
that was so unreliable a guide that some quoted it in reverse as
"Bright day, dark fly". The only sensible guide is "Match the
hatch", which is why imitative patterns are both more interesting and more productive.

'Choice of drifts or bank position is also important and
experience of *where* you may catch fish. But there is never any
rule of thumb about this. Each season is different largely
because different weather conditions bring different water
levels and different hatching cycles for the fly life. That means
constant study and adjustment to take account of these decisive influences.

'On tackle, however, you can make firm and lasting conclusions. To me the two most important items are the line and the leader. Floating line is not only a more satisfying method, but for 95% of the time a more successful one. It is in any case a popular misconception that to fish deep you must use sinking lines. By using leaded flies or nymphs and long leaders you can fish up to fifteen feet down with floating lines by letting the fly sink before starting the retrieve. Unless you prefer raking the bottom with fast-sink or leadcore lines – a form of fishing which is sometimes productive of big fish but has no appeal for me – you should use floating lines most of the time with the only alternative an intermediate line, which has the advantage that the fly keeps the same depth from the moment you start your retrieve.

'Weight of line is very important. AFTMA 7 is the most popular and rightly so. It is the most versatile for all stillwater work and for boat fishing or normal bank fishing enables you to cast as long as necessary. There are a few stillwaters, particularly those with concrete surrounds, where trout avoid the margins and very long casting is required for bank fishing making an 8 or 9 preferable. But these are not the sort of waters to attract me and my own alternative is to go down to a 6. On calm days, or when fishing dry fly, the line disturbance of the surface can be crucial with a lighter one making it less likely that you will scare the fish.

'Breaking strength of the leader is the next essential. On Chew and Blagdon visiting anglers are advised to use 7 lbs or heavier because of the size and power of the trout. But the regulars will be down to 5 lbs or less. In my own case I fish 4 lbs most of the time, though I appreciate that there's nothing worse than getting broken a lot, and that you should only go as fine as you can manage with confidence. But especially in calm, clear conditions or near the end of the season, when there are many well-educated trout about, fishing fine makes all the difference to the numbers I catch – thicker casts do scare fish away. So that's another thing for which I'm grateful to my father. He advised me early that it was essential to master the art of fishing fine without getting broken and the season of trial and tribulation in doing so was time very well spent. The secret is in a slow retrieve. The crucial moment is the take, since you should never get broken playing a fish in open water. If you are stripping through fast the fish, too, will take hard and fast, but a slow retrieve encourages quiet takes. The other essential is a strike which makes full use of the pliability of the rod tip to absorb the shock. That's much more satisfactory than technical expedients like high-powered gum.'

The small stillwater we fished together was Peter Lapsley's at Allens Farm near Fordingbridge, a delightful chain of little lakes with clear spring water typical of this chalk-stream area. Peter has developed the fishery to high standards with the rainbows averaging over two pounds and every opportunity to catch fish with imitative patterns – nymphs and dry flies are particularly successful. There's also a brook flowing past the lakes of the type which made Walton write: 'Hampshire, I think, exceeds all England for fast, shallow, clear, pleasant brooks and a store of trouts.' Unfortunately when we went there in late March the stream fishing hadn't begun, though I had a wistful look at it from along the wooded banks. With the water cold, the fish well down and no fly life yet visible, it was a time for sinking line and attractor flies, rather than nymphs.

But first there was an opportunity for lengthy discussion with Peter. He is a real enthusiast and a considerable authority on the technique of fishing these lakes. Apart from his writing, he is both a qualified National Anglers' Council Instructor and, even more prestigiously, a member of the Association of Professional Game Angling Instructors. Both these qualifications result from testing examinations probing knowledge of the whole range of angling techniques, of fly life and fly tying, and of teaching method. The APGAI syllabus is wider ranging and its standards the highest, though both qualifications are exacting enough. Peter was rightly outspoken about the desirability of good coaching for beginners: 'As with any sport the essential is to learn good habits at the start before adding to them your own special style as a result of experiment, experience and observation over the years. If you're lucky enough to be taught by fishing with very able anglers, that will start you right; but in general just learning by doing, or from watching a relative, is an unsatisfactory way of learning a complex sport. Industry found the old training method of 'sitting next to Nellie' to be ineffective because as often as not Nellie was passing on faults and errors as well as skills. It has long been established that some 20% of anglers catch about 80% of the fish taken on most waters. So if you get shown how to fish by one of that vast majority who don't catch many, then you have to be very bright and observant yourself not to remain in that group who catch relatively few. It's easy enough to learn to fish in a way which will catch you some trout – much harder to learn to be consistently successful in all conditions.

'Often people go through their fishing lives without appreci-ating some elementary points. Take nymph fishing here, for example. More than half the trout the really able nymph fishermen catch are taken "on the drop". As the nymph sinks slowly down before the retrieve is started – that's when most fish take it. But the leader then is slack and you're not in touch, so feel nothing. You have to notice instantly the slight move-ment where line and leader join and then strike swiftly and firmly. The trout will only mouth the nymph for a second or two before rejecting it, so your perception and reaction have to be razor sharp to hook them. But the vast majority of anglers I see don't think they are "fishing" until they start to retrieve, so they are not alert as the nymph sinks down and never even notice or know that it has been taken. Think what that means! They give themselves no chance whatever of catching perhaps 60% of the trout they rise! They may come in grousing that few fish were moving and that they've only caught one all day, whereas a better angler who appreciates the skill of fishing on the drop may in fact have moved no more but been off home early with his limit. In these clear waters it's often possible to see and stalk individual fish: you can see then how many which ignore a nymph retrieved past them, will take one as it spirals down on the drop, or can be "induced" to take by letting the nymph lie on the bottom then lifting it up in front of their nose as they circle past. Another lesson which can be simply demonstrated in these clear waters is the advantage of striking sideways. The natural reaction is to strike straight up. You can watch a trout mouth a nymph and strike it, lifting the rod straight up when you are certain you *must* hook it, yet often the nymph will come flying out without your getting a touch, or will grate against the bony part of the mouth and slide clear. Strike sideways and you *are* almost certain to hook the fish in the scissors with the best possible chance of landing it.'

Leaving nymph fishing, I asked Peter for advice on how to become ambidexterous when fishing – not only will it rest your hand during a long day if you can switch at will to the other, but on riverbanks there are often overgrown areas where it turns out to be much easier to cast under bushes if only you can use your weaker hand. 'The learning trick is simple and though it involves hard work it is well worth it,' was Peter's reply. 'Most right-handed fishermen, because they are experienced enough to cast a long line with their right hand, expect the same from their left immediately. Sooner or later, when they have a try with their left hand they give it up when they find it quite inadequate in comparison. What they have to recognise is that left-handed fishing has to be learnt from the beginning just as with the right – and that it will take a little longer. Instead of at once trying to cast twenty-five yards, they must start with the left by casting only a few feet. They have to learn a new casting rhythm for the different hand, then gradually lengthen their casting as they did when learning with the right. They will soon be reasonably competent and, again, it's a question of strengthening the hand by a lot of practice.'

Interesting as the talk was it was time now for some practical work. With Tony was his son John, another able angler who is already an England International and had just won third prize in France's first ever international flyfishing match staged on the Lac du Château at Dreux, some fifty miles from Paris. We each fished different lakes. I soon found that the rainbows fought well but without the fierce power of river fish. By the time we all converged on Pine Lake we had four apiece. A suggestion that the first to the limit of five should pay for lunch seemed to slow us all down a bit, but before long we all had our five good trout, averaging about 2½ lbs, for a splendid morning's fishing. There is, of course, much more to fishing than fish and this was yet another occasion when the attractive natural surroundings heightened our pleasure. So did lunch at the delightful Inn, the Rose and Thistle, at nearby Rockbourne, close to the site of a well-preserved Roman villa. I found that a few years before John had been in the Lancing College football team, which at once reminded me of an incident when I was still a keen soccer player at Millfield, before rugby took me over entirely. When I was there the school was just building a reputation in rugby and in the spring we also fielded a reasonable soccer team. Lancing was then one of the top soccer schools and for our games-oriented headmaster, Jack Meyer, a visit to it had the awesome importance of taking on Liverpool at Anfield! We ourselves knew little about their great reputation and cared less: on the way over I had bet the bus driver I would score, so when we had an early penalty I hurried forward to take it. With the ball in the net and the bet won, I had a carefree approach to the rest of the game. A minute from time we were losing 1–2 when we contrived a sweeping move – the centre came over low and I dived to head the equaliser. That left me feeling happy enough, but it was nothing to Meyer's ecstasy. When we returned he took us all out to the pub in triumph and later arranged a celebratory dinner. Quite a performance for just a draw!

Afterwards I asked Tony what general advice he would give about stillwater fishing, starting with the large stillwaters, to those, like myself, who were relatively inexperienced at it. This was his outline of basic principles: 'The first essential, as in all fishing, is not to be too proud or too shy to ask advice. The staff of the big stillwaters are usually knowledgeable and helpful; they will tell you where fish are being caught and with what patterns of fly. That's particularly important on big reservoirs, like Rutland or Kielder or Chew. If you don't know them the vast expanse of water can look very daunting – and if you don't start catching fish you're soon consumed with doubt as to whether you're fishing in the right way and the right place.

'Each fisherman has two basic decisions to make in relation to reservoir fishing which no one else can pre-empt for him. The first is whether cost is a matter of major importance or not – bank fishing is relatively cheap and is also productive enough that the cost per fish caught is usually much less. However, there are different attractions in boat fishing: of mobility, of avoiding crowds, of circumventing snags such as weed beds, of covering fish without long casting, and of a rather higher catch average. Some find bank angling more enjoyable in any case and some find it economically preferable. The individual who pays the money has to make the choice.

'Equally important, and again a matter of individual choice, is your fishing objective. For many this centres on catching a limit bag and this end justifies the use of any legal means! For others the means becomes almost an end in itself, and they are happiest fishing the method which most appeals to them, whether or not it catches most fish. Entries in the comment section of record books often reveal a vast disparity of view. After a bag of seven trout you may read: "One short of limit. Hard work," as if the business of fishing was just catching fish and it was as much work as sport. Another may run: "Enjoyable day, beautiful scenery, pleasant companions, and a brace of nice trout." For such a person the catching of fish is clearly only one part of the whole experience, of the total attraction. Only the individual knows what appeals to him, so general comments need to cover all effective methods from which the individual selects his own according to personal preference. It's probably true that if you indulge in everything from trolling (where allowed) to leadcore lining, to nymph fishing, and are competent in each method, knowing when to use which, you can catch a limit bag on 95% of the season's fishing days. But since the economics of "put and take" stillwater fisheries revolve on anglers averaging between two and three fish per visit – if a lot started fishing that way then either

the limits would come down or the price would go up, sub-
stantially.

'A long, strong rod of 10 ft 6 ins is ideal for such waters,
allowing distance-casting from bank or boat, helping you to
land heavy fish quickly, and to keep your line well clear of your
boat partner. Unless you have mastered the art of fishing fine
it's best to take no risk of being broken, so fish with 7 lb nylon
early in the season, coming down to 6 lb in the summer.
Whatever strength of nylon you use it's vital to buy the best;
Maxima is my current preference. The length of leader is vital
too: it should normally be a rod and a half long – some sixteen
feet – less likely to scare trout than a shorter one, and allowing
you to fish at a variety of depths even with a floating line. If you
do use long leaders you must join them to the line with a needle
knot, which will slip easily through the rod rings when you're
bringing a fish to the net.

'Love them or loathe them, the most successful new flies
since Skues pioneered nymph fishing are the Dog Nobblers
invented by Trevor Housby and developed by Sid Knight. For
those who like imitative patterns they are anathema: with the
shot head in the standard Nobbler, their bright colours and
waving marabou tails, they are unlike any actual living creature. But that waving tail *does* give a remarkable impression of
life and motion which attracts the aggressive rainbows, and
the shot head does make it easy to fish deep; while the
unweighted or lightly weighted varieties make it possible to
find fish at any level. The Dog Nobbler fishes even when not
being retrieved, its fluttering motion continuing as it sinks.
Certainly they have proved remarkably productive if fished
with a series of short and long pulls with an interval between
each. Part of the dislike of the Nobbler is indeed just because it
is so successful – it makes fishing at times seem too simple. But
when you first try a Nobbler, or indeed any heavily weighted
fly, be careful first to practise your casting well away from
other anglers and with the back of your head protected. They
require a quite different rhythm in casting, and until you
master it you're as likely to catch your own or your partner's

ear as any trout! With leaded flies you should drastically reduce the length of the leader.

'On reservoirs, as on many large lakes, bank anglers have one significant advantage: apart from the evening rise, the early morning, before the boats are allowed out, is usually the best time to find trout on the move. The main disadvantage is that there is rarely a general rise all over a reservoir; more often the trout are moving in particular areas, and it is much easier to locate them in a boat. Initial choice of position is therefore much more important for the bank man: if you don't know the reservoir well the dam is often a good place to start, provided fishing is allowed there. At least you will have easy casting into deep water and every chance of covering fish. Otherwise you want to head for significant features like promontories, or narrow bays round which trout will circulate, and the best fishing will often be where shallow water shelves into deep. On windy days look for sheltered areas and for preference fish from the lee shore: it's harder to cast out into the wind, but the trout are more likely to gather close by the bank to which it's blowing. If you find a place where the trout are rising stay there, otherwise keep on the move: it's more interesting and usually more productive than settling into one spot where little is happening.

'Many advise against wading, but when allowed in large reservoirs that seems to bring obvious advantages in being able to cover more water and cover it better. There are, however, some simple rules to be observed. Before you start wading, stand well back from the water's edge and fish the area close in to the bank. Always wade slowly, making as little disturbance as possible. Keep still when casting, and always net your fish where you are without wading back ashore.

'A number of boat fishermen prefer to anchor, and certainly that is the most productive method for fishing near the bottom with fast-sink lines and large lures, such as a tandem Christmas Tree, on which many big browns are taken at Rutland. Unlike the bank angler you can pick your spot, never be crowded, and fish direct into deep water all round the boat. But to me it's a monotonous way of fishing and I prefer to keep on the move. The exception, as with bank fishing, is when you hit a shoal of rising fish or a very productive area: then it does pay to anchor and enjoy good sport over a period rather than drift past with only one caught.

'Fishing the drift in the traditional loch style is the most pleasurable way of tackling big reservoirs. You can quickly drift a number of likely areas until you find one where you spot fish rising, or start moving them yourself, and then concentrate there. It pays always to be alert for hopeful signs, whether bending rods in distant boats or concentrations of birds, indicating a fly hatch. On most days in these wide waters there are dead expanses with a number of "hotspots" between them, so it pays to find where the action is and stay there. On windy days short-lining and bobbing a dropper near the boat may pay dividends, but more often a reasonably long cast and a retrieve right to the boat will raise more fish. The reason is simple: many more trout will see the flies, and rainbows often like to follow for a distance, taking only as the fly is about to lift off.

'The retrieve needs to be faster when you drift before the breeze than it does in bank fishing. The boat is taking you down on your flies at some speed so a slow draw will only keep pace with it, barely moving your fly at all. And except in nymph fishing, it is movement that most attracts and triggers the trout to attack. In strong winds the drogue is a great help in slowing the boat, essential to covering the water properly and moving the fly properly without having to strip in line at frantic speed. In these conditions feeding fish are often to be found in the wind lanes on the edges of the oily water. When the breeze is very light chasing it can be a waste of time and energy, but if there is a sizeable and lasting ripple in any small area, fishing the edges of it should also bring a good basket of trout. Flat calms on bright sunny days are the severest test. You're fishing as if anchored and have two main choices. Fast-sink lines and fishing deep will sometimes be productive, since the trout stay down on such days. But nymph fishing with the floating line may be even more successful, provided you use long leaders, cast without disturbance, let the nymph sink down to where the fish are, and ensure that your cast has had fullers earth or perma-sink applied to make it sink easily and without drag.

'One place which on reservoirs is worth a try at most times, but particularly in the hot dozy summer days, is by the aerator. The "boils" round it usually harbour many trout and often offer the best prospect. In the long hot spell of 1983 there were times at Bewl Bridge, for instance, where those who fished its large "boil" area usually had limit bags, while elsewhere a brace was hard to come by. Sometimes trout can be taken there close to the surface, but in hot weather they are more often found deep down by using a weighted fly and a fast-sink line.

'On most reservoirs at most seasons there are moving fish to be seen, so finding them should be a first priority. If you can do that and then "match the hatch" in your patterns of fly or nymph, you can cover them with hope. That's the most skilful and interesting form of fishing, though, of course, to be a fisherman for all seasons and conditions requires greater versatility. But you can have reasonable success on reservoirs by concentrating on just one method. For instance, if you fish a Dog Nobbler on a sinking line you should catch some fish most days – if you go to the right places. To be consistently successful, though, and for maximum interest and enjoyment, you need continually to adjust and adapt and to be alert to changing conditions. That doesn't mean trying too many variants or wild experiments. For example, while there are thousands of patterns to tempt you, a range of ten wet flies should be more than enough. If your box has Soldier Palmers, Grenadiers, Dunkelds, Wickhams Fancy, Invictas, Black and Peacock Spiders, Muddlers, Greenwell's Glory, Black Zulus and Black Chenilles, you have more than enough for any eventuality. For lures or Nobblers you need only the primary colours of Black, Orange, Yellow, or White, though I have also found Green and Olive effective. For nymphs, buzzers, and dry flies you need only a small range, with a Daddy Longlegs, to be fished dry or just subsurface, to round off an all-round collection. Then you will find that during the whole season you probably only use a quarter of those!

'You can widen your knowledge by reading and talking with successful anglers, but don't take it all on trust. Evaluate technical advice against your own experience. If you experiment sensibly, and log or remember the results of your own experience, that's the best way of all to improve. But it does pay to watch an expert early on. Small stillwater tactics have some similarities to bank fishing on large reservoirs, but there's much more to it, particularly in those lakes where you can see and stalk many of your fish. I learnt to catch larger numbers and bigger fish by watching and taking advice from Alan Pearson, the expert in these waters on catching big trout, and by marrying that in with my own experience. For these smaller waters Alan's main principles do indeed lead to better catches. The points he drummed in to me were simple enough, starting with the need to give yourself the best chance of spotting fish. The first time I watched Alan was at Church Hill Farm Fishery in Buckinghamshire. For an hour or more he wandered round without casting, peering through his polaroids for a fish large enough and active enough to interest him. Then he stopped to chat with another angler. "See anything?" he asked him. "Nothing yet," was the reply. "How about that five-pounder swimming round just below your feet?" so surprised the less observant fisherman that he asked Alan to have a go for it; a few minutes later the large rainbow was in the net.

'As with dry fly fishing, Alan usually casts only to seen fish, yet rarely, if ever, will these be surface risers. He's after the heavier ones, cruising slowly and feeding deep and the fast movers he ignores, for they're a waste of time to chase. His particular skills are in the spotting of fish and in getting his leaded fly or nymph rapidly in front of their noses, involving nice calculations of depth, the speed of sinking, the length of cast. Spotting the fish is an art in itself. Apart from wearing drab clothing and moving quietly along the bank to avoid scaring fish away, the essentials are polaroid glasses to cut out glare and make fish more easily visible, and a peaked cap to shade the glasses.

'Alan holds all the records for UK rod-caught freshwater fish taken on fly. His rainbow record is 19¼ lbs, his Brook trout 5 lbs 13 ozs. Both were taken at Avington, close to Winchester. Since his prime targets are fish of 4 lbs or over, Alan may spend most of the day looking and very little of it casting. For me that requires too much patience, so my own routine is to try and catch two or three by more conventional methods and then go looking for a big one when one short of a limit – if I get that far!

'Like Alan, I will always have a large net for any fishery where big fish are a possibility. On the much rarer occasions when I catch one I now remember to draw it out on to the bank rather than strain wrist and net handle by lifting it straight up out of the water. That was learnt the hard way. At Avington I was playing a 7¼ lbs cheetah trout when I found I had left my net on the bank the other side of a tree which it was impossible to circumvent. A kind lady fishing nearby lent me hers. When what was then the third largest cheetah ever caught was safely in its folds, I lifted the net high in triumph. But the unexpectedly weak metal handle promptly buckled under the strain, and it was an odd looking net that I handed back with profuse apology!

'On small stillwaters you rarely need to cast long; I fish always with a double taper floating line. Alan, with his concentration on larger fish, cuts this in two and uses a short eleven-yard line attached to a shooting head of flattened nylon monofilament. This is not primarily to give distance in casting but to prevent the heavy weight of yards of line dragging the hook out when a big trout makes a long run. It also means that many more yards of monofilament backing can be carried on the reel to cope with even the longest surge of a monster trout, but the backing needs to be strong. I was amused to see Alan himself caught out when fishing with a large party of us on 8th July 1983, prior to the special celebration service in Winchester Cathedral to mark Izaak Walton's tercentenary year. I'm not sure what the old master would have made of the antics of the present master catcher of big fish. With a French television crew filming him, Alan hooked a rainbow of about 13 lbs. Hard though he plays his fish, this one took him well down the backing, which broke at a weak point. The fish stopped running, the coils of line and backing sank slowly to the bottom. Undaunted Alan stripped off, dived in, recovered the line, found the fish still on, and landed it! He then obliged the late-arriving TVS film crew with an "action replay" which kept them happy, though it did little for the chances of neighbouring fishermen.

'Imitative patterns are best for such waters and none is better than the Mayfly nymph, appropriately leaded. Two other points I picked up from Alan are to play the fish by hand on any type of lake, rather than off the reel and to have plenty of reserve tackle in the car when visiting a small stillwater, but only take a minimum to the water with you. A few flies and a spare reel of cast is all you should want, rather than clutter yourself with unneeded alternatives. You can keep these in your pockets but I prefer a back pack – you can also carry the fish in this without interfering with your mobility or casting – unless you catch them Pearson-sized!'

There was much to learn and admire when fishing lakes like Lapsley's or Chew Valley. I enjoy stillwater trout fishing enough to appreciate Tony's enthusiasm for it and the enormous attraction it has for hundreds of thousands of flyfishermen. But for me the call of the salmon rivers remains irresistible when I have any choice.

9

Coarse and Match Fishing

By personal choice almost all my fishing has been game fishing. Of course, this has involved techniques such as worming and spinning which are also common to coarse fishing, and it is certainly no prejudice about method which has kept me from enjoying this part of the sport except on very rare occasions. 'Coarse' fishing refers to the fish caught not to the techniques used (which can require the finest tackle, the highest skills), and still less does the term refer to the anglers themselves!

Some coarse fish, such as perch, are bright of colour, graceful of form; some, like the pike, have a deadly symmetry, with a look of functional perfection as a predator. But I was brought up on trout fishing, early captivated by the beauty of that marvellous fish, which only sea-trout and salmon can rival; and only the grayling, more game than coarse fish, comes close for me to their attraction. The rest bring me little pleasure in capture, hardly seem a prize worth striving for. The special attraction game fish have for me may be inborn or bred from those early blissful days on trout streams. Certain it is that the attraction is deeply ingrained. When I was taking part in the television Fishing Race a long period of coarse fishing was followed by a trip to a far northern river full of grayling and trout. The perceptive Swedish guide remarked, after watching me flyfish for them: 'Before you were just a rod-holder, but now you are *really* fishing.' The presence of game fish had indeed brought me alert and alive, since to me they were so much more desirable a prize.

Television is the medium which has most frequently involved me in coarse fishing. Ulster's, for instance, provided me with a coarse fishing experience which was a remarkable mixture of the comic and the nerve-racking. Their choice of company was inspired – the pairings were Chris Tarrant and Ian Heaps; Billy Connolly and Ray Mumford; Jenny Hanley and Stan Piecha; Frank Carson and Max Winters; myself and Tony Scott. The choice of venue and the timing, however, could hardly have been more unfortunate. The river we fished was an experimental stretch near Enniskillen which turned out to be poorly stocked with fish by Northern Ireland's high standards, and only with small ones at that. The chosen days were those of continuous rain; its depressing effect was deepened by the extreme tension in Ulster following the death of Bobby Sands. When we suggested moving to a more productive beat we were informed that *They* had let it be known we were safe where we were, but if we changed by even a few miles there was no guarantee what might happen. We opted unanimously to stay put. For our final night in the Manor Hotel so warlike was the scene, with searchlights intermittently illuminating our room and helicopters hovering overhead that some of us felt it more prudent to sleep on the floor rather than on an exposed bed by a window.

The Tourist Board may have been misled by catches earlier on the River Cam, where we fished. Like several rivers in the area, it is only really productive when the fish move out of the lakes as spawning time approaches; once they return only a small resident population remains in the river. In an extreme case you may get record weights taken for a couple of months and then find that for the rest of the year the river is almost barren of fish except for a few brown trout. So choosing your time is important if you fish a new river in this region! If you don't check when large catches are made you may be disappointed, as we were, that a water doesn't live up to its reputation. So poor was our catch indeed that Stan Piecha and Tony Scott were taken off for a brief filming session early one morning on a nearby lake. In a few hours' pre-breakfast fishing they had 70 lbs weight of varied species to provide shots which were then skilfully interwoven to make the 'competition' look rather livelier on screen than it was in practice. But, as Stan Piecha and other experts commented, even if the fishing was disappointing the general atmosphere in the party made for two very enjoyable days' fishing.

The discomforts of the weather, the unusually poor fishing, the anxieties of the time, though, were more often forgotten in the non-stop flow of jokes from the humorists. Billy Connolly is such a keen fisherman and concentrated so hard on our 'competition' that he was more serious than usual, but nothing for a moment stemmed Frank Carson's stream of stories and ribald comment: 'Where I started fishing we needed a dipstick rather than a water gauge. So dirty was the canal that the fish thanked me for catching them . . .' On and on it went, keeping us amused even at the dreariest moments. Nothing could stop him. Chris Tarrant was in the next room to him in the hotel and woke at three o'clock one morning to hear Frank, through the wall, still telling jokes – to himself – and laughing uproariously at his own wit!

When I was pegged next to Frank Carson it was hard to concentrate on my fishing as the flow continued: 'There was this chap in a pub. He was told his wife had died while out in the garden pulling a cabbage for his lunch. So what did he do? Opened a can of beans instead . . .' There was just one five-minute period of silence when Frank's lips were as well sealed as those of most of the spring salmon I have tried to tempt. His fishing was far from being as fluent as his story-telling and a terrible tangle developed in his line. With the cameras on him Frank was briefly too intent on unravelling it to talk. He made up for it that evening. Billy Connolly had relaxed at last and was entertaining us with some hilarious imitations of local celebrities. In walked Frank and without pause or permission took over the act. By the look on big Billy's face that was one of his most courageous, if not one of his most popular turns!

Chris Tarrant and Ian Heaps were the winners of the

competition round which Ulster Television wove the programme, with myself and Tony Scott the runners-up. Ian
Heaps, of course, is one of the half-dozen Englishmen who
have won the individual title in the World Freshwater Championships, though the England team as a whole has never been
successful, in over a quarter of a century of these competitions
which attract some twenty-five nations to enter and large
crowds to watch. Ian told one story to illustrate the quick-
thinking that may be necessary in such professional contests.
In 1975 he won the World Championship in Poland. One of
the rules of the competition is that not only may you not fish
beyond your own marked area of twenty-five yards or so, but
you may not let any hooked fish go beyond it, otherwise it does
not count. Early on Ian hooked a large bream and it was soon
clear that on his fine tackle he had no hope of holding it within
his area without being broken. The judge at his back, however,
could only tell the whereabouts of the fish by the line cutting
through the water. Ian thrust the tip of his rod deep down into
the river and played the fish far below the surface. He landed it
and the bemused judge let it count, as neither he nor the
spectators were certain how far it had gone. In all sports, it
seems, gamesmanship is inevitable in top-level competition,
even in fishing.

But that incident typifies for me the expertise of such top
performers in the coarse fishing world. I was impressed not
only by the technical skill with which they used groundbait to
draw fish to them, but even more by the neatness with which
they handled a whole range of equipment and baits, and the
speed with which they adjusted to changing conditions. My
own tackle tends to be stuffed haphazardly into a bag when
game fishing. Theirs was always kept in perfect order, despite
the complexity of different baits, different floats, different
weights and hooks. And they were remarkably swift and
competent in handling a variety of rods, from poles with a
fixed line to swing-tip rods and the float-fishing, in which Max
Winters and Tony Scott specialised. Such fish as we caught in
Ulster were mainly small roach, but on other occasions I have

admired the skill with which large fish are hooked and landed on the finest leaders down to 1 or 2 lbs. At the top level these anglers remind me of Artie Jones and his perfectionist approach to worming. The weights have to be exact, the depth exactly measured, the bait carefully chosen and swum in the most attractive way at the exact level at which fish are feeding. Perfect presentation is the aim, with a remarkable difference in the catch between experts, with the experience to get it right consistently, and the haphazard angler who only gets it right occasionally.

For the visitor to Northern Ireland there is often a strange atmosphere about fishing. For the most part you are absorbed by the excellence of the sport in a country which regularly beats all records for numbers of coarse fish caught and which also has some fine game fishing. You are absorbed, too, by the beauty of an unspoiled countryside and the natural friendliness of the people, so it takes you the more by surprise when sinister overtones of the continuing strife suddenly intrude. That was Tony Pawson's experience also when he went to fish Lough Melvin, one of the clearest, cleanest lakes in Europe and a flyfisher's delight, with its profusion of bays and islands, its change from rugged rocky shoreline to sheltered areas of reed beds. It's a shared lough in the sense that the border runs through the middle, with a dispute also as to whether the best fishing is on the Southern or the Northern side.

The lough has a remarkable diversity of trout – four different species present in quantity. There's a profusion of gillaroo trout close in to the rock-strewn shores; with their bright yellow bellies and vivid red spots, these plump fish are the most colourful of all trout. The browns are present all over the lough, and shoaling in deep water are the sonaghans – the slim torpedo-shaped trout which leap when hooked and fight in the lough's still waters with all the power and panache of a sea-trout aided by a fast current. Finally, there are feroxes – not the usual ugly fish with large head, ferocious jaws and tapering body, but sleek, well-proportioned fish that many rate as a separate species. At times, too, there can be good runs of grilse and salmon into this fascinating lough.

Hurrying to sample its attraction, Tony forgot how close it was to the troubled border area and was taken by surprise to round a corner straight towards a blockhouse. In huge red letters a vast signboard commanded him to stop on pain of being shot. Jamming on the brakes, he sat in eerie silence for some minutes before getting out to investigate. Beyond the blockhouse was a second fortified sentrypost; two paras were chatting outside it, machine-pistols slung across their chests. They looked askance at him before one said, 'Sorry we didn't notice you. But you're the first person who's ever stopped at that sign.' Later in the evening came a further example of how close are normality and nightmare in that suffering land. Back at the hotel in Belleek, his Irish host suddenly noticed a trout rising in the Erne River as it flowed past the garden wall. At once his rod was out and he was casting to it. Tony then spotted another, rising persistently close in to the wall. Stalking it carefully then crouching behind a large bush, he began to flick the fly over it. When the trout took he rose to his feet to play it and was immediately aware of another person making even better use of the cover. A soldier lay full length on the other side of the bush, machine-gun to shoulder and pointing unwaveringly at a house on the far bank, towards which Tony could now see others creeping. The trout was hauled out, the fishing session ended. Returning to the bar for a reviving drink he joined the crush of Americans who had come in busloads for an exhibition of Belleek's famous black china. Commenting to the landlord on the room's pleasant aspect he was told it had just been rebuilt in record time after being bombed for the third time. 'Whenever we appear too prosperous *They* come and do us over,' said the owner cheerfully. Wondering if *They* were also eyeing the crowds of Americans, Tony decided it would be prudent to spend most of his time far out on Lough Melvin or Lough Erne where, as added incentive, trout up to 19 lb have been taken spinning and many heavy fish on fly at mayfly time.

It was on Lough Melvin that the first flyfishing international between England and Ireland was staged, as long ago as 1937. Many may dislike the idea of such competitions in a sport intended primarily for relaxation – they feel it ought to be free of the pressures such matches can generate. But I've no scruples about fishing the occasional one. Most of my angling friends take some pleasure in proving their skill by bettering anyone else's catch, and it's a very short step from the one-upmanship of scales on spectacles or forehead, to the test of actual competition. I think it's even more demanding to compete in front of cameras and in a branch of the sport at which you are not particularly experienced.

That, to a degree at least, was my experience when I was talked by Clive Gammon into entering the television Fishing Race. This was the second series, the first having attracted great interest in its format of three pairs fishing against each other for a continuous three-day period, with the aim of catching as many different species as possible and as large specimens. Mostly it was to be coarse fishing, so I was relieved to be paired with an all-round angler of Clive Gammon's skill, but first I arranged with the producer, Mike Begg, to have some lessons in coarse fishing to brush up on the technique required.

We went to Bosherston Lake in Wales. Clive Gammon gave some tuition in ground baiting and techniques of maggot fishing, and also had me practising live and dead bait fishing for pike, something which was to come in useful in Lapland later on in the series. Coarse fishing was not so different as to give me any real problems, but sea-fishing was entirely new. I only had time to realise that it was not as simple as it looked and that I had no hope to learn much about it in time! We had a couple of days fishing out from Saundersfoot and Tenby, and my confidence was boosted when I caught a 40 lb tope. But I knew I would just have to follow any advice Clive gave me and hope for the best.

Though I know I *am* competitive when I fish it's usually quite unconscious. Mostly it involves simply a trial of skill between me and the fish and the elements, with a pride in achievement, plus the drive which gives fishing its special appeal to man, who is by nature a hunter. There's great pleasure in using your skill to overcome adverse weather conditions, to cover difficult water, to avoid snags, to master a wild fish in a heavy stream, and frustration also when you fail. Instinctively, though, you do compete – in the nicest possible way, as Kenny Everett would say – with any companions with whom you are fishing. A blank doesn't upset you if *they* don't catch anything either, but it becomes very depressing if you find the others have been hauling them out!

Still, I didn't feel unduly pressured when the television cameras were focused on me and I was expected to catch something in unpromising conditions – or at least to look a competent performer without mistakes or tangles. So I didn't start the Fishing Race feeling very competitive or desperate to win the prize of The Golden Maggot. But gradually it got to me. I hadn't expected that we would do well, because my own lack of experience in the main elements of coarse and sea-angling was likely to prove too much of a handicap, even with Clive's all-round ability to help us. When, near the end in Sweden, I found we were leading both the previous victors, Ian Gillespie and Jim Gibbinson and the other pair, Kevin Linane and Terry Eustace, I was elated by the thought of winning. So when a disastrously bad final session on the sea pushed us back into second place I was correspondingly depressed, feeling as bad as if Wales had just been narrowly defeated by England at Twickenham. For most of the time I had been absorbed in the fishing, the competitive aspect only latent in my mind: it had seemed no stronger than the urge to catch fish on any normal day. By the finish I knew it had been much more powerful than I'd realised.

The pressure, too, had been much greater than I'd expected or experienced on previous television occasions, but it wasn't pressure of competition or of public exposure to the cameras, of which we soon ceased to be conscious. It was the sheer physical and mental pressure of continuous fishing and driving, of uncomfortable conditions and of lack of sleep. When the Race began I was at my fittest; when it ended I was more drained and exhausted than after any rugby international. For some of the older contestants it was a shattering experience. People tend to under-rate the concentration required in fishing, and that alone can wear you down over a period if you have no real rest.

Of course, all this was just what the television men wanted, since one aspect of the programme was to show our reactions when tired and confronted with unnatural problems. So they hoped for an occasional acrimonious remark or display of temperament – even from equable anglers! Indeed each team was encouraged to play practical jokes on the others to stimulate the odd explosion of anger; sometimes the commentator, Ian Wooldridge, would himself arrange for something strange to upset us for the amusement of viewers. Yet some unexpected incidents were not carefully planned, nor at all disagreeable: there were, for instance, the topless lady canoeists whom we could easily forgive for disturbing the water as they paddled over to enquire how we were getting on. By contrast, however, there was one very fraught occasion. Clive and I were enjoying some excellent pike fishing on a Lapland lake in the northern leg of the competition. Our spinners had already extracted a number of large specimens when Clive called that he was into a really big one. As he played it a canoe came close, manned by a very aggressive Laplander who appeared likely to break the cast with his paddle as he gesticulated at Clive. His face was deeply lined, burnt mahogany by long exposure, his belligerent expression heightened by missing teeth and the tanned leathery skin. Clive, threatened with the loss of a specimen fish, was quite angry himself but so consuming was the Lapp's rage that Clive soon changed from furiously waving him away to pacific words and gestures, which did nothing to calm him. Our guide sidled up to warn Clive that the Lapp was shouting that we were fishing in hallowed water, sacred to his ancestors, and unless we went away he would attack us. He did indeed start waving a lethal-looking knife. Clive was on the point of cutting and running when the Lapp's face cracked into a wide tooth-less grin; we found our guide was also doubled up laughing: it was another Wooldridge-arranged prank. Clive took it in good part, particularly as he netted his 12 lb pike, and as he himself had pulled the best coup of the contest. Before the competition started Clive flew to Stockholm, knowing that we all had to fish in front of the Royal Palace there and knowing, too, the time when Gibbinson and Gillespie were due to tackle that section. Over the radio he had it broadcast that two world-famous English international anglers would be there at such and such a time with the object of passing on their secrets to any schoolchildren who wanted fishing instruction. The two were so mobbed by enthusiastic youngsters they had little chance of fishing successfully!

The trip had started badly for me. We had crossed to Gothenburg by boat with all our gear stored in the caravanette which was to be home once we were in Sweden. Clive had brought large quantities of specially prepared maggots, the favoured bait for coarse fishing. Looking at even a few mag-gots makes me feel queasy, and the sight of a bucketful of them, all squirming and wriggling, did nothing to make me feel happier about having them as travelling companions for the whole of the competition. When the caravanette was unloaded and we started to check our equipment I was revolted to find that the maggots had spilled out and crawled into every corner. Keen coarse fishermen can handle them as affectionately as they would a pet, but nothing would induce me to sleep in a vehicle with undiscovered maggots in many a cranny. From then on I insisted on hotels or the open. And a sneaking suspicion that this had been deliberate sabotage made me wary of our rivals!

Even without such interruptions this competition proved to be the most tiring few days of my life. Each team had to fish in south Sweden, in Stockholm and up in Lapland, so between each section we had four hundred miles or more of travelling followed by eighteen hours of fishing from dawn to midnight. By the fourth day, when our spirits were at a low ebb, we also had our most taxing assignment. At three in the morning, unshaven and bedraggled as a couple of tramps, we huddled over our rods with the grandeur of Stockholm's Royal Palace at our backs. In the chill morning air our hands were frozen, no fish were biting, and dangling our maggots in the river fifteen feet below was as dreary a form of fishing as could be imagined. The still, deserted streets came momentarily alive as a couple of revellers made their unsteady way home. Almost unbelievably they turned out to be two Welshmen who recognised me, despite the beard, and began talking rugby. For once I had surprised Ian Wooldridge and his camera crew: The last thing they expected just before dawn in Stockholm was Welsh voices calling 'Where's the game, Gar?' 'Can we have your autograph?' When the sun came up and the street filled we began to catch fish in plenty, the fine tackle and choice maggots now irresistible. But it was a weird experience and to me a travesty of fishing, like sitting on the Embankment and dropping the bait in the Thames amid the roar of traffic and the petrol fumes.

The previous day had given me a memorable experience in the clear crystal waters of a Lapland river. We had snatched some sleep in a log cabin after the flight up and the hospitable Lapps had revived us with a rich meal, but tired as we were we couldn't keep away from that beautiful stream, starting by fishing for fun in what was meant to be a rest period. The dam of a hydro-electric scheme prevented salmon getting up that far, but the water was alive with monster grayling. The British record is under three pounds but between us we caught and returned a score of them heavier than that. Clive shook off the largest we hooked and later regretted not netting and weighing it, for he was sure it would have run to over five pounds. Amid the grind of that Fishing Race, these were hours of pure pleasure – the clear, sharp air, the beautiful scenery, the inviting water, the game fish which fought so hard in the fast current provided refreshment for the spirit. It was a place where I wouldn't have minded being marooned – and I nearly was, for the pick-up helicopter broke down. But, in the gloaming a small sea-plane came gliding in to make a hazardous landing and whisk us from that quiet, peaceful place to the bustle of Stockholm.

When we headed out to sea from Gothenburg for the final hours of the contest Clive and I were still leading, but in choppy water the sea-fishing was not very productive or pleasant. Clive and I added few to our species and were overhauled by the expertise of Kevin Linane in this kind of fishing. There was, however, one great consolation. Ian Wooldridge had gone out of his way to produce pressure situations which would test our temperament to the limit. That they certainly did, but they also developed in us an infuriated attitude towards him. As we went sleepless and became ever more tired it was maddening to see Ian refreshed and taking his ease, sipping gin and tonics, and looking so aloof and disdainful. He had confessed to having no understanding of or liking for fishing, and the more obvious he made this feeling the more it grated on us. So we all had a laugh to ourselves when he swiftly became a victim of the swell – to see the superior being leaning over the rail with his face an unhealthy green was balm to us all. The more he suffered, the happier we were: after all his tricks, the sea had levelled the score.

The Fishing Race had been quite an experience and though not one to be repeated, for me it was worth it just to meet Clive Gammon. He taught me so much in such a short time and I enjoyed his flow of controversial ideas and expert advice. There was so much more I wanted to learn from fishing with him, but hardly had our friendship sealed than he was off to America, where he continues to fish and write so authoritatively. So for me the race had no happy ending.

10

Competitive Flyfishing

The Fishing Race and the Irish experience were far removed from the normal types of competition which are now so popular, in flyfishing as well as among coarse anglers. It's not a form of fishing in which I have any desire to participate often but I appreciate its excitement for some, and so was interested to hear Tony Pawson's views. As one who has fished in home Internationals and in two World Flyfishing Championships Tony has experienced a variety of formal competitions: 'At the first-ever National Stillwater Conference, organised by the Salmon and Trout Association, I was invited to put the case for competitive flyfishing being a reasonable part of the sport. Brian Clarke expressed the views of those who believe it contrary to the whole spirit of angling as a relaxed recreation for individual enjoyment. It soon became apparent that this was regarded as perhaps the most important debate of the two-day conference, since there are strong opinions on the subject, particularly from those who dislike the idea of any competition or who fear that flyfishing competitions might become as highly professionalised as has some of the coarse anglers' match fishing.

'To me there is no question of having to defend or "justify" such competitions, which are in any case far too well and too long established now for their continuance to be in question. The first annual river competition was organised in 1831, the inaugural year of Britain's first fishing club, the Ellem Club, formed by some Berwickshire and Edinburgh gentlemen, many of them regular fishermen on the Tweed or Loch Leven. It took place on the Whiteadder River. The account of that initial event recorded: "The members, having roused themselves by time, proceed in their several ways. At seven o'clock, the hour appointed for the commencing of the competition, a spectator from an adjoining hill might trace hickory and casting lines flickering through the mist in many a distant glade. About four o'clock in the afternoon the competitors might be seen emerging wet and weary from the different valleys which surround the tavern, each oppressed with the weight of an unusual quantity of trout."

'The Scots took over from that date, taking the lead in developing flyfishing competitions to their present level – the main part, as one Scottish international put it to me, of the Scottish Angling scene. Scotland organised the first National Flyfishing Competition, held on Loch Leven more than a hundred years ago. The Scots too were involved in the first international event when challenged by some regular and expert English fishermen on Loch Leven. That was held in 1928 with H.R.H. the Duke of York as the England captain elect. His team of twenty won by the narrowest of margins though he himself was unable to be present. Such interest did the contest arouse that three years later Wales and Ireland sent "spectator" teams to fish alongside the formal England *v* Scotland contest. Both countries were sufficiently excited by what they saw to enter teams themselves in 1932, so the full home internationals began between teams of sixteen from the four countries. More than fifty years later the contests are going even stronger – though the teams are now down to fourteen there are two internationals each year instead of one, and the venues change between the four countries instead of being confined to Loch Leven. Selection, too, is more "democratic", with the teams taken from the winners of countrywide eliminating contests rather than chosen from an illustrious few.

'First you have to qualify for the National Final by coming in the top twelve in the eliminating heats in one of five English regions, in my case the South. It then needed a placement in the top sixteen in the Final to bring automatic selection for one of the two internationals in the following year. By coming seventh out of sixty in the Final at Chew in 1978 I qualified for the spring international which, by coincidence, was also to be fished at Chew. That Final gave me a good lesson in how keen the competition was and on the need to stay alert throughout the eight hours. The boat partner with whom I was drawn came from another region, and at first neither of us had any success. As we drifted close to a boat where a good fish had just been netted he called across to enquire the fly on which it had been taken. "Ace of Spades" was shouted back. That black fly is, in fact, often effective in catching rainbows and was no doubt the one used but neither of us had then heard of the pattern and my partner was convinced he was having his leg pulled. Almost immediately he himself caught a fish on a Dunkeld and the neighbouring boat now enquired what he had been using. "Bloody Jack of Diamonds" was the gleeful response!

'Late in the day we were fishing where little was happening when, in the distance, we noticed several bending rods in a number of boats drifting across from the Lodge area to Denny Island, so we sped over to try our luck there. At that point my partner had four, myself only two, but on the new drift my Soldier Palmer and Wickham's Fancy became irresistible – at one stage three good rainbows hooked in only five casts. That finishing burst was enough to win me my England place.

'Even the practise was taken very seriously, with our team having several get-togethers before the two special days' practise prior to the match itself. These were our instructions from our captain, John Ketley, for one of them: "We will meet at Chew at 9.30 a.m., pair off into boats and fish the day through until 6 p.m. We will stay locally and fish on Sunday again until 6 p.m. followed by a team meeting before we drive home. It will be a friendly couple of days and we will be responsible for our own expenses. Chew is one of the most consistent fisheries in the country because it has hardly any large areas of deep water. Flies or lures seem to work equally well, and apart from the first fortnight of the season, sinking lines are seldom used by the regulars. Stephen Pope, a member of our team, has fished the lake most days of his life and is a great believer in the floating line, a long leader, a thirty-yard cast and a fast retrieve. His team of flies usually has a Grenadier on the bob (sometimes three of them!), with a Silver Invicta and a Mallard and Claret of maximum competition size."

'If you play the percentages that is indeed the method which may work most often in such competitions. But each day is different, and no one technique is infallibly assured of success. On the day it was the Scots, fishing a more traditional Loch style – bobbing the dropper on the wave, and using flies such as the Fiery Brown – who proved easy winners. Their outstanding fisherman was Brian Peterson, the individual winner with nine trout weighing 17¼ lbs. Early on Brian hooked two at once, a two-pounder on the dropper and one of about four on the tail fly. The line was pulled out at such speed it burned his fingers. The larger fish then straightened the hook and departed, though the smaller one was safely netted.

'Representing your country in fishing, as in any sport, engenders considerable tension and pressure, particularly for the inexperienced. If you're having a bad day there are eight unrelenting hours in which to worry about it, the anxiety becoming more acute each time the opponent in your boat nets a fish. For the member of our team in Brian Peterson's boat it was a long, long day: while Brian always seemed to be playing fish he had a blank. Like me, he was experiencing his first international and an agonising experience it proved. My own was much more relaxed. The friendly rival in my boat was Roy Jones, a fishery manager from Bettws-y-Coed and a previous Brown Bowl winner. As advised, I fished with a floating line cast far and drawn fast. He fished a slow sinker, and short-line, working the dropper close to the boat. I hold my breath as trout swirl at my flies, following but not taking, but it's his reel which sings first and he lands a nice brown, caught, he tells me on a Green Peter. My box doesn't contain the effective Irish fly, but I switch to a small Muddler on the point, promptly taking a rather larger rainbow. With a fish in the boat the shadow of the dreaded blank dissolves and the rest of the long day is enjoyment. We fish with total concentration, swap the occasional story and hook fish at intervals. By the 6 p.m. finish, we have both caught two more and each lost three others, so satisfaction and disappointment are nicely balanced. At least I have followed my captain's instructions to catch a heavier weight of fish than my boat companion. Within half an hour the swift weigh-in is completed – and there is a great cheer from the Scots, as their average of 8 lb of trout apiece gives them an easy win.

'John Ketley had earlier won an international with the heaviest bag ever taken in the first fifty years of internationals. It was at Llyn Trawsfynydd in 1978: "On our practice days we had been asked to avoid fishing a particular area: I assumed it was because it was likely to fish particularly well, and told my team to fish there as long as possible, but control of the boat changes every two hours and not many were able to get their boat companion's agreement to this. In the end, only three boats stayed there all day and they were the three boats which had the heaviest catches.

' "The match day dawned wild and wet with a near gale blowing. These were conditions in which big trout were moving and the nine I had weighed one ounce under twenty-one pounds. Practically every fish came in the wildest part of the drift, right on the shoreline. Once I had a four-pound-plus fish on the top dropper and simultaneously one over three on the point – all in two feet of water. My Irish boat partner showed great sportsmanship by picking up two nets and landing both fish for me, while our young boatman struggled manfully as the boat beached among the weeds.

' "In really rough conditions in shallow water there is nothing like a small Muddler on the point for the big rainbows. It also helps keep the other flies off the bottom. On the top dropper I fished a Blackie (a local fly which is very like a Red Tag) and as this broke through the crashing waves, rainbows surged through the shallows in pursuit, back fin out of the water in the eagerness to seize it. This was a thrilling way in which to win the coveted Brown Bowl." '

Tony Pawson adds: 'The rules for such competitions are based on maintaining the purest traditions of loch-style fishing from drifting boats and most formal competitions follow this same pattern. Their increasing scope and popularity is well illustrated by the National Club Championship, launched by the Salmon and Trout Association and Benson & Hedges in 1982: the response was so overwhelming throughout Britain that many more applied to enter than the organisers could accept. Balloting restricted entry to sixty clubs; a Leicestershire team won and a Northern Irish one was runner-up. The following year a hundred and sixty teams of six competed, with nearly a thousand anglers involved, and the number was expected to double again the next time. Apart from the more formally organised competitions there are a mass of informal events or specialised events like the night sea-trout competitions on the Teifi. Even an elitist body like the Piscatorial Society runs its flyfishing competitions for grayling, while the Flyfisher's Club, too, has entered a competitive team on special occasions.

'Acceptance, then, is so widely based that organised competitions are more likely to increase rapidly than to wither away as some of the major casting competitions have done, notably the Usk Valley Competition which was once a major event, but became too poorly supported and too expensive to run. For casting is just one peripheral skill in the art of angling. As Walton put it: "Angling is an art – or at least it is an art to catch fish." Casting is no substitute for the total art.

'What objections can there be? Some argue that fishing is all right so long as the contest is only between man and fish, but that it's quite wrong for there to be a contest between man and man over the catching of fish. That's a spurious argument, like saying it's all right to do something for fun but not for a purpose. Once individuals decide that angling appeals to them there is no ethical difference between fishing solely for fun and being covertly or overtly competitive, *provided* the fishery's rules are kept. And in competition the rules are normally stricter, the standards higher.

'That is very relevant to the next point advanced against competition – that it may pressure you to catch lots of fish when they are feeding and easy to take. Certainly you tend to fish more intensively and perhaps try that little bit harder to catch trout than when you're on a pleasure outing, but most formal competitions now adhere closely to the rules of the International Flyfishers' Association which specifically provides for competitions to be at the hardest time of the day, that is from 10 a.m. to 6 p.m. It's the pleasure anglers who swarm out at dawn and dusk when the trout are often feeding confidently, and are simple to catch; the purist dry fly anglers who *only* fish for trout clearly on the feed.

'The same stringent attitude applies to equipment and methods. Formal competitions have kept in the main to the high standards of loch-style drift fishing, with the size of fly limited for practical purposes to a No 10 hook and overall dressing of 15/16ths of an inch. It is the pleasure stillwater anglers who rake the bottom with leadcore lines and flies larger than a Devon Minnow, or who strip large lures, or fish out of the back of a drifting boat to give the same effect as trolling – or indeed indulge in trolling where this is allowed. On many of England's "put and take" stillwaters it is the competitions in which thousands indulge, which encourages them to practise the more refined and interesting types of flyfishing rather than to succumb to the "limititis" bug, trying to get their limit by any legal means (or even illegal ones in some cases).

'The next argument against competitive fishing is that limits are sometimes waived for these competitions and large numbers of fish caught. That does sometimes happen, but most competitions are still fished under exacting conditions which make a big basket much harder to achieve. In the home Internationals, for instance, most captains tell their teams that if only each of them catches a brace of keepable trout in the eight hours their team are likely winners – and as often as not that's the case. In most Internationals the venue is a natural lake like Loch Leven, or Loughs Melvin, Conn, Corrib or Sheelin, with no limits except size, even for pleasure fishermen. Competition rules often increase the local size limit by an inch or two precisely to prevent a borderline trout being kept and then found to be below the legal limit. And in "put and take" stillwaters the normal limits are highly variable and based on economics rather than ethics. Should the ideal limit be four, as at lakes like Avington, or five as at Lapsley's, or eight as at Chew, Blagdon, Grafham, Rutland, Bewl and the like? And is eight really the limit, when on many waters anglers can purchase a second, or even a third ticket, and so go out and get sixteen or twenty-four in the day? And what is different with stocked lakes like Eyebrook, which has no limit except those the fisherman's own ethics or ability impose on him?

'The final worry was expressed that "It would be wrong for people to make money and a reputation out of catching trout, as happens in coarse match fishing." That, too, is very wide of the mark since the main competitions are amateur, have been so for over a hundred years and are likely to remain so for the foreseeable future. Indeed, until very recently, those who *did* make money and a reputation out of flyfishing by writing about it, instructing professionally or making profit from selling tackle, were barred from international competition even if they, like everyone else, were ready to accept the cost of a couple of hundred pounds or so involved in the eliminators, the practise days and the international itself.

'My own feeling has always been that there are many people who will not wish to enter competitions – and why should they? Equally, there are many who do – and why shouldn't they? Too often anglers take a puritannical attitude, expecting everyone else to fish the way they do, but this is a sport for individual enjoyment, and if the rules of a fishery are kept and it's happy to stage a competition – that's fine. Man never can resist a challenge, anyway, so there are always going to be many who will enjoy it, even though there may well be a slightly higher proportion who would never dream of entering. But a majority of those who disapprove of formal competition are in fact competitive in their own way. Douglas Sutherland summed it up nicely in *The Salmon Book*: "Even those whose life is match fishing are no more and no less competitive than the Rolls Royce set who migrate annually to the exclusive salmon beats and spend the rest of the year boasting of their triumphs, or bemoaning their failures. They are all brothers of the angle under the skin." They are indeed, and decrying "competition" is as old-fashioned as decrying nymph fishing. But fishermen do love an argument!

'Regular match fishing wouldn't appeal to me, but I can recognise that it develops coarse fishermen with skills far above the average. The World Freshwater Championships attract teams from over twenty countries, with more than a hundred expert anglers involved. No luck then in the regularity with which the French team wins, or in the achievements of some individual Englishmen. In 1982 at Stratford on Avon, England came second to the French but Dave Thomas caught the heaviest weight of any individual in the team event and then went on to win the individual title by doing the same again the following day. The next year, when it was fished on the Newry Canal in Northern Ireland, Kevin Ashurst announced in advance that he would emulate Dave – and did so, jumping into the canal to celebrate his individual victory! The high degree of knowledge and instinct needed for such performance was summed up for me by Dave Thomas: "As an experienced match angler you must never let misfortune destroy the plan and rhythm of your fishing. In the Stratford World Cup I was playing a good chub early on when the crowd alerted me to a branch likely to float into my line and break it. I avoided the danger skilfully enough by pushing the rod tip down deep to let it drift over. Then the fish came off at the net for no apparent reason and the sigh of the large crowd round me deepened my own disappointment. But I didn't let it affect my concentration and was soon netting some other big chub. If you compete at the top, attention to small details is vital. There

Fishing in the Eastern Transvaal in South Africa.

Gordon Lesinger, the gillie on The Hawthorns at the Junction Beat on the
Tweed, nets the fourth salmon of the morning in front of the television cameras.

Tony Pawson nets a rainbow for me in Pine Lake at Lapsley's Trout Fishery
in Hampshire.

are more than a dozen items to get exactly right – the type of
float, the size of hook, the weights and so on. Get one shot out
of place and on hard-fished waters it may be the difference
between a blank and 10 lbs of fish. But instinct is important
too. There are perhaps a hundred options in the way you fish –
with what method, in what area, at what depth and with what
bait. Fish react differently at different times and so must you.
You may start catching them one way then they dry up on you.
To be a winner you have to choose right at the start and choose
right again whenever you need to change.

'In a different form, this view was exactly echoed by the
most outstanding competitive flyfisherman it has been my
privilege to watch. Bob Draper has such outstanding skills that
though he fishes his eliminators in the exceptionally strong
Midland area, he qualified for thirteen out of fourteen succes-
sive internationals and made a major individual contribution
when he led England to a win in four of his first five internationals as captain. Part of his secret of success is very long
casting, using an eleven-foot rod, but he stresses the need to use
instinct – to have green fingers, as he puts it – and adapt at the
right moment when the mood of the trout changes. For this he
instances an occasion on Loch Leven when he won the individual award, the Brown Bowl, and his team won the International in 1977. Bob was deprived of the first hour's fishing –
usually one of the best times – because the gillie stranded his
boat on the shallows round St Serf's Island. Annoyance no
doubt added power to his casting and by one o'clock he had six
good trout, fishing deep. Nothing then stirred for a long
period, but at the start of the final hour he noticed the odd
trout moving, switched to a floater and had five more for a
total bag of 16½ lbs. It was Bob, too, who exploded the
received wisdom that Loch Leven trout were most easily
caught by short-lining with "wee doubles", size 16: he proved
that the best catches came fishing long with the largest size the
competition allowed, size 10.

'For me the main attraction of entering the occasional
competition has been to fish with experts like Bob and to learn

from them. It has introduced me to a whole new range of fishing friends and fishing ideas. In the seven years in which I have, on average, spent ten days a year practising or competing, I've learnt more than in all the previous fifty of pleasure fishing. Through it I have had contact with outstanding Scottish fishermen like Eric Campbell or Brian Peterson; with Mervyn and Victor Williams of Wales, the only two who have ever twice won the individual prize in home internationals; with overseas anglers like Pierre Affre (Mr Eurofishing) of France, Jean Zender of Luxembourg, and other very able and interesting European fishermen. The friendships and the lessons have been of prime importance, but of course another good aspect of competition fishing is that you test yourself against the highest standards. In normal fishing circumstances you comfort yourself, when others catch more, by thinking that you were taking it easy, or had bad luck, or a long lunch break, or the worst beat, or whatever. When you've tried your hardest for eight hours under equal conditions, you're left without illusions or excuses!

'Competition does sharpen and improve your ordinary fishing, too, even if only because it makes you much more aware of all the items you ought to check, like the sharpness of the hooks or the strength of the knots, so that you leave less to chance. If you enjoy competition, as most of us do, the matches themselves can bring a new dimension to your fishing. Each fish you catch is a very special fish, not just another to be soon forgotten. Equally, whereas the experienced angler shrugs off the loss of a trout as of little moment in an ordinary day, in competition the loss is as acutely felt as if it was the first fish he had ever hooked. All the competitions in which I have fished have enriched my experience and knowledge.

'Though winning or losing is a matter of intense importance to competitors there are times when competition can be completely relaxed. One of the annual contests between a House of Commons team and a team assembled by the Salmon and Trout Association is a good example of this. There were two teams of eight involved. The House of Commons team was an all-party affair – on this occasion comments such as 'Your leader is up a tree,' related to a rare fishing misfortune rather than the usual exchange of bantering insult. One of the Association's team, Bernard Cribbins, also had his priorities right: under considerable pressure to withdraw from the event and to join instead the press and television launch of The Theatre of Comedy, he solved the problem by going fishing while the cameras back in London focused on a lifesize cardboard cut-out of him, propped in the back row amid the other comedians.

'This was the third such annual contest to be sponsored by Amoco and staged at Bayham Lake near Tunbridge Wells in Kent. It was typical of the keeness of the MPs to take part that John Mackay named a lifeboat in Oban just five hours before he clocked in for the get-together on the evening before the start. That looked like turning into another all-night session as the MPs debated at length every rule of the contest without reaching their usual clear-cut decisions. For anyone seeking omens about the election result the match presented only a confused picture. The House of Commons team all lost, which might have presaged a hung Parliament. The Tories had more members in the team (more seats?), but the most successful pairing was Labour's Roy Mason and John Golding.

'Fishermen, like farmers, have a reputation for complaining about the weather. On this occasion a little moaning was fully justified: the two previous contests had suffered from a gale and a heatwave, and now there was a flood to make fishing difficult. Bayham is one of the most beautiful fisheries in the country, well-stocked with good-sized trout, and with a river to add variety to the lake fishing. Now, however, its torrent added an unwelcome suspension of mud, turning the lake coffee-coloured and putting the fish down.

'Amoco had undertaken to donate £20 for each pound of fish taken; the teams had agreed a suitable charity, selecting The National Association for Disabled Anglers. In the circumstances they did well to achieve an Amoco contribution of £1200. The Salmon and Trout Association had thirteen trout weighing 44 lb with Peter Tombleson, Director of the National Anglers Council, the day's most successful angler – he had five rainbows, including one of 8½ lb, for a total weight of 19½ lbs. These were taken on a Black Chenille and, like most of the fish caught, came from the Cascade Pools in the morning session. Alan Pearson inevitably had one large fish in his three, and he and I were the only ones to catch a trout in both sessions. Bob Church also had a nice rainbow and Roger Daltry a small one. The Parliamentarians were led by Sir Geoffrey Johnson-Smith and managed six fish weighing 17½ lbs. Roy Mason and John Golding caught half of them and another two were taken by David Swatland, Chairman of the Salmon and Trout Association, who was substituting for the indisposed Sir Charles Fletcher-Cooke. It was appropriate that John Golding should be the most successful of the House of Commons team, for he represents Charles Cotton country. Cotton's master fishing companion, Izaak Walton, was a royalist and High Churchman who would certainly have approved the defeat of the Parliamentary forces in his ter-centenary year. This would no doubt have provided him the 'merriment' he loved but, as a very kindly man, he would also have wished them all better luck in enticing the electors than they had had in snaring the fish. Indeed, when the cheque was presented in the House of Commons some months later, all who fished had duly retained their seats; since Walton also equated anglers with very honest men, that was perhaps fortunate for the country.

'The Izaak Walton Commemorative Tournament, part of the tercentenary celebrations took place in July 1983. It was staged at Patshull Park for over twenty teams including some from Eire, Scotland, Wales, France, Spain and Luxemburg, as well as one selected from England's Disabled Anglers team who fished on equal terms and finished high up. Patshull Park's Great Lake was an ideal setting for what was primarily a social occasion with the Lakeside Hotel catering admirably during the long lunch break and the gathering at the weigh-in. David Tooth, President of the Patshull Flyfishers Club, ensured that all ran smoothly. Terry Thomas made the draw and launched the competition in style, and with ebullient characters like Brian Geraghty of Ireland and Moc Morgan of Wales taking part there was never a dull moment on or off the water.

'The sweltering July heat had made fishing difficult that season on most stillwaters, with the trout torpid and down at the bottom. Patshull was no exception though, as always, well stocked with fish. The competition was from boats which could be anchored, and there was no limitation on flies or method other than the normal rules of the fishery. Even if the occasion was mainly a social gathering, the two three-hour sessions were as usual fished with the dedicated concentration that the challenge of competition always inspires. The French were the winners, a success due largely to Dr Kron whose nine fish weighing 13¾ lb proved decisive. What was his secret on a day when a team of such fishermen as Bob Church, Arthur Cove and local expert Alan Barker managed just two fish between them, both caught by Bob? My son John was at the other end of the boat watching him catch nine while he hooked only four. His view was: "Dr Kron is a very good long caster and with an instinct for where fish may be. He had the advantage of a practice the previous afternoon allowed only to overseas competitors. From that he had deduced where we were likely to catch fish and he had four in the morning. But that success didn't stop him making lengthy enquiries at lunchtime, and then suggesting a different afternoon position at the far end of the lake, where we did find more fish than in the morning. He also had highly successful patterns of fly not in common use here. The two on which he caught were a salmon fly of the Connemara Black type (shades of the early stillwater fishing at Blagdon when the large trout were usually taken on salmon flies!), and a French concoction, the Escargot or Snail Fly. This looked like the enlarged head of a Muddler without the body and had some resemblance to a "Pellet" fly, so perhaps it was especially attractive to recently stocked fish." Certainly Dr Kron's fishing was attractive enough to the trout for him to win the individual prize and France the team prize –

an event happily recorded by the French television crew as well as our own. The second individual prize went to a highly skilled lady, Maggie Vaux, who had seven trout weighing 9¼ lbs, and second team prize to the Salmon and Trout Association.

'Missing on the day was Bob Draper, the really outstanding English competition angler who makes nonsense of any thought that fishing is mainly luck. Known as "Mr Consistency" because he has three times won the English National as well as being runner-up on other occasions, he also won the Brown Bowl at Leven in 1977. He has often been England's top rod in international competition; indeed, under his leadership England won four of the first five contests in which he was captain. Over the years he has learned to adjust for other situations a technique of long casting which was highly successful in stocked reservoirs. On natural Irish waters, though, it brought him little return at first, for the trout there rise so fast and reject the fly so quickly that the long caster is at a disadvantage in hooking them; but now he has adapted to find an effective method there too. He is the epitome of the expert angler, combining technical skill with an unerring instinct for catching fish.'

But would old Izaak have approved of Bob, or indeed of fishing competitions? Certainly! His definition of the true angler: 'What makes an angler? It is diligence, and observation, and practise, and an ambition to be the best in the art, that most do it. I once heard one say, "I envy not him that is richer or wears better clothes than I do. I envy nobody, but him, and him only, that catches more fish than I do." And such a man is like to prove a true angler; and this noble emulation I wish to you, and all young anglers.' What a formidable team he and Charles Cotton would have been.

11

The Game Fish of New Zealand

Rugby tours had an added zest for me when they involved the chance of fishing in far waters, so what could rival a Lions tour to New Zealand where the football and the trout fishing are so superb? When I was playing for the Lions there was only fleeting opportunity to try out the legendary Taupo Lake, but opportunities were more plentiful for Clem Thomas and myself to explore it when we both went to commentate on the 1983 tour.

Taupo is a vast lake, full of large rainbows. As the fame of the water grew so did the numbers visiting it, who felt they must catch fish by any means, however dull, and in the lake itself now much of the fishing has degenerated into trolling. Many expeditions are offered on the terms that if no fish are caught the money is returned, and the easiest way to ensure that fish are caught on Taupo is to take visitors trolling. That way the boat and its owner do the real fishing – hunting out and hooking the rainbows – so no skill is required from the angler except in the playing, which can, admittedly, be very exciting and testing. When I was with the Lions team in 1971 I was taken out one day in a boat and had to troll large flies behind, and there was a sense of satisfaction in landing rainbows up to 5 lbs which had plunged and leapt and stripped off yards of line even in those still waters. But there was no sense of having hunted them myself or of winning any battle of wits with them: I spent more time admiring the scenery than concentrating on fishing. For just to be out on Taupo is an experience. There's the invigoration of the clean, fresh air, the wonder of the clear, aquamarine-coloured water in which you can watch every move of a hooked trout, and above all there's the wild, romantic setting appropriate to a lake created in the distant past by a cataclysmic volcanic eruption.

According to Maori legend one of their great priests or *tohungas* created the lake by hurling a totara tree into wasteland where it pierced the ground and water gushed forth. Geologists can put you straight on that, but the Maoris' name for the lake is much to be preferred to the one now on the map; they still call it Taupo Moana – the Sea of Taupo, to describe both its great size and its rôle for rainbow. To them it is indeed a sea from which the trout migrate up river to give marvellous flyfishing in the Toṅgariro, the Tauranga, the Waitahanui, the Waikato, and a rush of smaller streams. There were no natural trout in the water when the British first decided to stock it, and the introduction of those first trout sounded a fascinating adventure story on its own.

There were many failures before trout were at last successfully introduced into New Zealand in 1867. Roe was shipped out from England in 1864, having been stripped from trout of Itchen, Tweed and Severn to produce a truly British collection of ova. Refrigeration on sailing ships was unknown but the problem was solved by piling blocks of ice ten feet high on the two hundred or so boxes of fertilised ova, which had been packed in moss above layers of crushed ice and charcoal. Primitive that might have been but it was effective enough to ensure the ova survived the twelve-week voyage to Melbourne and transportation to Tasmania, where the first brown trout were hatched. Once established there, they were introduced into New Zealand between 1867 and 1870; within a few years fishing for brown trout in rivers there was flourishing.

The remote Taupo Lake had its first brown trout in 1886, put in by the Auckland Acclimatisation Society which had also sponsored the introduction of rainbow trout to New Zealand from California just three years earlier. Before long the rainbow had become the dominant species; an active, aggressive fish and one which may spawn any time in the year, it proliferated at the brown's expense. All talk of Taupo now is in terms of rainbows – and magnificent rainbows at that – though there are still large brown trout to be taken. In Taupo's early years, when the browns were plentiful, they had been caught up to 25 lbs, but the voracious rainbows soon took over, decimating the shoals of the lake's indigenous fish, the *kokopu* and *inanga*, and the freshwater crayfish, the *koura*. As food stocks declined and the rainbow population exploded, average weights came down over ten years from 8¾ lbs to 3½ lbs in 1918. Then heavy netting to reduce rainbow numbers restored a natural balance in which exceptional growth was again possible. Since 1924, however, weights have again steadily declined to the present level. For the oldtimers 3½ lbs may be a small fish; for me, the hooking of such trout, descended from steelheads and with all a steelhead's surge of power, was one of the great fishing experiences of my life, when they were taken in the rivers round Taupo on my recent visit.

Fishing, perhaps more than any other sport, lends itself to the idea that the golden years were in the past, that the golden days are always the week before or the week after you are on the river yourself. Often that's just idle talk, but when we were told of a period when the Taupo trout *averaged* over ten pounds, compared to the 3½ lbs of today, that talk is backed up by the records. There are even stories of throwing back anything under double figures when old anglers recall the *annus mirabilis* of Taupo in 1924: then, for the only year on record, the average was 10½ lbs, with rainbows up to 20 lbs not all that uncommon. Much of the information no doubt came from O. S. Hintz's famous book *Trout on Taupo*, a classic of the 1950s. Hintz is a keen sportsman who came over to England to report the New Zealand cricket team's tour in 1931; he must have enjoyed that first Test win of theirs in this country just fifty-two years later.

Just before our Lions tour, Taupo hosted the centenary celebrations of the introduction of American rainbows to New

Zealand. The Mayor of Taupo, Clem Currie, had no doubt that Taupo was the right focal point to represent all New Zealand. As he said, 'The fishing is so good, the rainbow has symbolised Taupo for so long – this is the logical place to celebrate on behalf of the whole country.' So universal was that view that eight cabinet ministers attended the activities there. One highlight of the week was an international trout fishing tournament, the fourth to be held at Taupo. In the previous three annual contests, with some 450 anglers taking part in each, an overall total of 2420 trout were caught, averaging 3 lb 11 oz.

What now is the view of that great Taupo authority, O. S. Hintz? At the centenary he commented: 'The golden years are in the past, but Taupo remains a notable trout fishery by any standards.' Nostalgically, he recalled the largest rainbow ever caught there: 'One of 37½ lbs was hooked and played by a Maori fisherman in the little Mangamutu stream which flows into the Waitahanui. My old Maori friend, Awhi Northcote, used to say, "Big fish! We had to cut it in two to weigh it!"'

Nothing so large is likely now, but there may be very big browns lurking round Taupo, as elsewhere in New Zealand. In 1982 a fifteen-year-old, Nigel Remnant, caught one of 24¾ lbs in the Oreti River in South Island. Nigel's first attempt to land it cost him his net – the giant brown trout bit clean through the mesh as he tried to lift it out.

My kindly guide in 1983 was Graham Thorne, a tough opponent in the All Black teams of 1967 and 1969. He was covering the tour for the New Zealand Broadcasting Corporation and we had many a yarn to swap on the matches of those two years. Knowing my love of fishing, which they share, Graham and his father, Norman, arranged a trip to Taupo, not to the main lake, with its trolling, or to the popular rivers like the Tongariro, but to one of the smaller streams flowing into it, the Waitahanui. On the way we looked at the famous 'picket fence' area at the mouth of that river where anglers stand shoulder to shoulder on a sandbar whenever the trout are running up the river: there's barely room to cast without hitting your neighbour, and if you hook a fish you have to step back and with rod held high work it rapidly down to the end of the line to land it. And when the rainbows are really running you have to queue for that too!

Graham had judged well the type of water that would most appeal to me. The Waitahanui River was not too different from the upper reaches of some Welsh rivers: there were fast runs and quiet glides, overhanging trees which promised trout lying beneath, and lush vegetation on the steep, winding banks. Two things only were beyond my previous experience – the clarity and colour of the water, and the fighting quality of the fish. For a time it was the water which fascinated me and the fact that though I could see every pebble on the bottom, the large trout we knew to be there were so hard to detect. Then my Red Rabbit fly was seized by a rainbow and the shock of that take threw me right off balance. Graham came rushing back to me, having seen me stagger and thinking I was in danger of falling in. No twenty-pound salmon I had hooked in the past had ever taken with such savage force, and I was glad to have 8 lb nylon as cast or I would certainly have been broken. The rainbow took off like a demented sea-trout, jumping, tearing off line, impossible to control in the narrow river; the reel was never silent for a second. If the fish wasn't stripping off line I was trying hard to recover it, with the early rush having taken me down to the backing. When Graham netted the rainbow at last it was hard to believe there was a 3½ lb fish rather than one double that weight. No wonder weight alone is not enough for New Zealanders.

The Wildlife Service of the New Zealand Department of Internal Affairs produces a condition factor chart for New Zealand trout. In their view: 'The condition of a trout is more important to most fishermen than its length or weight. There is nothing more thrilling to the angler than the landing of a deep, chubby, hard-fighting rainbow and for complete satisfaction it is important that this condition can be recorded, rather than just the weight.' I hadn't come across that concept before, but

THE CONDITION FACTOR CHART
As used by the Internal Affairs Department

TROUT CONDITION FACTORS GENERAL TABLES

The condition of a trout is more important to most fishermen than its length or weight.
There is nothing more thrilling to the angler than the landing of a deep, chubby,
hard-fighting rainbow and for complete satisfaction it is important that this condition
can be recorded, rather than just the mere weight.

WEIGHT IN GRAMS

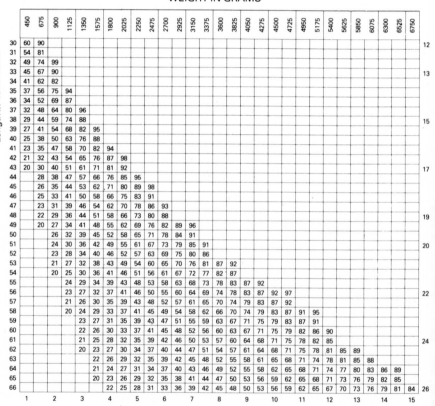

Length (cm)	450	675	900	1125	1350	1575	1800	2025	2250	2475	2700	2925	3150	3375	3600	3825	4050	4275	4500	4725	4950	5175	5400	5625	5850	6075	6300	6525	6750	lbs
30	60	90																												12
31	54	81																												
32	49	74	99																											
33	45	67	90																											13
34	41	62	82																											
35	37	56	75	94																										
36	34	52	69	87																										
37	32	48	64	80	96																									
38	29	44	59	74	88																									15
39	27	41	54	68	82	95																								
40	25	38	50	63	76	88																								
41	23	35	47	58	70	82	94																							
42	21	32	43	54	65	76	87	98																						
43	20	30	40	51	61	71	81	92																						17
44		28	38	47	57	66	76	85	95																					
45		26	35	44	53	62	71	80	89	98																				
46		25	33	41	50	58	66	75	83	91																				
47		23	31	39	46	54	62	70	78	86	93																			
48		22	29	36	44	51	58	66	73	80	88																			19
49		20	27	34	41	48	55	62	69	76	82	89	96																	
50			26	32	39	45	52	58	65	71	78	84	91																	
51			24	30	36	42	49	55	61	67	73	79	85	91																20
52			23	28	34	40	46	52	57	63	69	75	80	86																
53			21	27	32	38	43	49	54	60	65	70	76	81	87	92														
54			20	25	30	36	41	46	51	56	61	67	72	77	82	87														
55				24	29	34	39	43	48	53	58	63	68	73	78	83	87	92												
56				23	27	32	37	41	46	50	55	60	64	69	74	78	83	87	92	97										22
57				21	26	30	35	39	43	48	52	57	61	65	70	74	79	83	87	92										
58				20	24	29	33	37	41	45	49	54	58	62	66	70	74	79	83	87	91	95								
59					23	27	31	35	39	43	47	51	55	59	63	67	71	75	79	83	87	91								
60					22	26	30	33	37	41	45	48	52	56	60	63	67	71	75	79	82	86	90							
61					21	25	28	32	35	39	42	46	50	53	57	60	64	68	71	75	78	82	85							24
62					20	23	27	30	34	37	40	44	47	51	54	57	61	64	68	71	75	78	81	85	89					
63						22	26	29	32	35	39	42	45	48	52	55	58	61	65	68	71	74	78	81	85	88				
64						21	24	27	31	34	37	40	43	46	49	52	55	58	62	65	68	71	74	77	80	83	86	89		
65						20	23	26	29	32	35	38	41	44	47	50	53	56	59	62	65	68	71	73	76	79	82	85		
66							22	25	28	31	33	36	39	42	45	48	50	53	56	59	62	65	67	70	73	76	79	81	84	26

Bottom pound scale: 1 2 3 4 5 6 7 8 9 10 11 12 13 14 15

WEIGHT IN POUNDS (APPROX) : ½ POUND INTERVALS

By courtesy of the Wildlife Service. NZ Dept. of Internal Affairs.

The factor is a comparison on a length to weight ratio and is expressed thus:

Imperial: $\dfrac{\text{Weight}}{\text{Length}} \times \dfrac{100.000}{1}$

Metric: $\dfrac{\text{Weight}}{\text{Length}} \times \dfrac{3612.8}{1}$

However for the majority of catches these days the table laid out above will give a ready answer

Further copies of the Condition Factor Chart are available on request to: Kelly (Rotorua) Ltd. P.O. Box 1441, Rotorua.

it can make an interesting addition to the record book to use the chart opposite.

The method of fishing was ordinary downstream casting, with large wet flies of patterns specially developed for New Zealand rainbows. The Red Rabbit had its streamer of rabbit's fur and a body that was said to resemble the look and colour of trout ova. Fishermen prefer to think they are using 'imitative' patterns but I suspect this is not 'imitative', just a large attractor fly which excites the rainbows' aggression. The plume of rabbit's fur had a nice wavy movement in the water which no doubt gave the impression of life to trigger the feeding instinct. Many colours of rabbit flies – red, green, blond – can prove successful, as can some fly patterns which take rainbows over here, such as Muddlers of various colours and Matuka flies.

I was very much at home on the Waitahanui River since the technique I used was not too different from that of river fishing for salmon or sea-trout; at least it proved one effective way of taking these wonderfully sporting fish. For the purists and the floating line specialists, another method can be equally productive. Some of those I saw catch fish were casting upstream and using nymphs fished just below the surface. In the faster water it was often a problem to see when the nymph was taken, but unless they tightened immediately the nymph was rejected, the chance gone. Those fishing this method have to concentrate on the join of line and leader to detect the moment the nymph is slipped in and the movement of the line halted. Then you need to make the instant sideways strike to hook the fish in the scissors. The New Zealanders made things much easier for themselves than I have seen any British anglers do: they added a touch of luminous paint at the join so that even in dazzling sunlight any change in its steady downstream movement was instantly visible. That was a clever dodge, which might prove even more successful in our own murky climate.

Clem Thomas had told us he was going to try the famous Tongariro River, noted for its swift current and hard-fighting trout. When he met us later this was his account of his fishing there and his wider experience of game fishing on previous tours:

'It was Zane Grey who so aptly called New Zealand 'The Anglers' Eldorado' and so vividly portrayed its great adventures with the giant trout, swordfish and shark so plentiful in the land of the great white cloud. My own experience is pale in comparison with Zane Grey's massive expeditions to the Bay of Islands and the Tongariro River which became such a magnificent obsession and brought him peace in his middle age. Nevertheless my encounters with the rainbow trout of the Tongariro and my game fishing in the Bay of Islands are equally as vivid in the matters of high excitements and the perception that in New Zealand the fisherman can find his Holy Grail.

'I have never fished in areas of more exquisite beauty than the Bay of Islands and the coastline to the north and south. The myriad volcanic islands are a treasure house of visual joy and a marine paradise. As you cruise through them you are followed by cavorting porpoises and dolphins and you can see acres of schoolfish shimmering on the surface. This paradise of 144 islands is situated on the east coast of the northlands, some 160 miles north of Auckland's international airport. The climate is perfect and the game fishing season for some species is all year round. I have even fished for marlin in June and July, but it's not advisable to go there at that time, for it is their mid-winter. Yet even in those months the hotels serve barbecue lunches.

'The most prolific game fish are the Striped marlin, which go to 500 lbs; the largest caught in the Bay of Islands is 455 lbs. Stripies here are the biggest in the world and are renowned as magnificent fighters, largely caught on 50 lb breaking strain lines. Only in Peru do you find them that large but it is New Zealand that holds many of the world records for the species. They usually appear in December during the post-spawning migration to New Zealand waters where there is an abundance of food to put condition back, and remain until June. Squid, saury and mackerel are the most common prey but marlin are also known to feed on Mako and Blue Shark. There are also the Pacific Blue and the Black marlin. Neither is found in anything like the numbers of the striped variety, and can be caught only in the summer months from January to April. Catching one is the thrill of a lifetime. They do go to 1500 lbs but the New Zealand record for a Pacific Blue is 1017 lbs and for a Black, 979 lbs. Occasionally, too, the rarest and most prized of all game fish, the Broadbill, are sighted in these waters, but they are reluctant feeders. The New Zealand record stands at 673 lbs.

'Unhappily commercial long-line tuna boats are now catching two and a half times the average recreational catch of between six and seven hundred fish. Inevitably this will put the most terrifying pressures on these marvellous game fish, something which is causing much concern for their survival.

'There are three species of shark, the Mako, Thresher and Hammerhead, caught in New Zealand's waters all the year round. The ferocious Mako is the most abundant; between seventy and ninety are caught in the season. New Zealand's records are 106 lbs for a Mako, 802 lbs for a Thresher and 467 lbs for a Hammerhead. Although they are far less prized than swordfish, catching a big shark is still a colossal excitement. The other game fish caught round the Bay of Islands are the Yellow Fin Tuna, now coming back in greater quantities, and the light-tackle winter fighter, the Yellow Tail or King Fish. Colin Deans, the Scottish hooker who was controversially kept out of test series by Fitzgerald of Ireland, at least proved that he was the best hooker when it came to fish: during the Lions' stay in the Bay of Islands he caught a 27 lb Yellow Tail to provide the Lions with their traditional regulation fish photograph! Although my own efforts on that occasion were fruitless, apart from catching a Kahawi, which resembles a large sea-trout and which we used for bait for marlin, a boat-boy made the day for us by diving for crawfish – on the way home we enjoyed a succulent supper of fresh crawfish and butter.

'It is quite simple, although it is advisable to do it well in advance, to book a game fish boat. These are luxury boats ranging from thirty-four to sixty feet and equipped with toilet, cooking facilities, refrigeration, flying bridges and comfortable live-aboard facilities. The maximum number of rods is four and anglers share the time. Each boat has a current survey certificate and is equipped with top-quality tackle; there is also continuous radio contact with the charter office and with the other boats, who will always tell you where the fish are running. Boats on day charter usually leave Pahia, Russell or Waitangi at 8 am and return at 5.30 pm, but I advise the live-aboard cruises – there is nothing more enjoyable than a fish supper and a few beers in one of the beautiful bays watching a sensational South Pacific sunset!

'The skipper and the deckhand are expert in finding fish and many fish are caught by people who have never game fished in their lives. Different skippers employ their own fishing methods. Usually on the way out to the main game fishing grounds off Cape Brett and Piercy Rock you fish for Kahawi or Trevalli, which are silver fish of the size of a large sea-trout; the ideal bait is about 5–8 lbs and you use them as bait for drift fishing or trolling. When trolling they often use two brightly coloured teasers, skipping about thirty or forty feet from the stern while your bait skims the water between and behind the teasers. The knack is not to spin the bait so that it will not twist your line.

'My favourite skipper is Eldon Jepson, who is part-owner of the *Lady Lynn*, a forty-six foot wide-beamed bridge-decked cruiser with a covered flying bridge. It has deep freezers, refrigerators, hot and cold water, radar, automatic pilot and television and is powered by twin-engine Perkins diesels, ideal for live-aboard fishing, Eldon is a Kiwi to his seaboots and he sold his farm in middle age to take up game fishing. He is a marvellous yarner and his fishing and farming stories when you are not fishing are delightful enough to offset any disappointments when you don't catch a big fish. But if you go out with him for three days your chances of catching a marlin are very high indeed.

'The Bay of Islands area is redolent of New Zealand history.

Bob Tennant with a 71lb salmon of 44 inches, caught with herring strip at River's Inlet on the Campbell River off Vancouver Island.

With Rhys and Owen and a fine April fish on Graham Evans's Golden Grove on the Towy. Sadly these beautiful early fish — this one was $17\frac{1}{2}$lbs — are now few and far between.

With Tony Pawson and his son John, and a morning's catch of rainbows at Lapsley's.

It is an important Maori region – nearby is the Treaty House where the Treaty of Waitangi was signed. Not surprisingly, there is plenty of good accommodation, ranging from the luxury Waitangi Hotel to smaller motor inns or, if you like, you can hire a holiday apartment in Pahia or on the island of Russell, with the Bay of Islands Swordfish Club on the water-front, which is so hospitable to overseas anglers. In the evening the boat skippers congregate there and you hear fishing stories to end all fishing tales. Radio Northland broadcasts daily the fish caught during the day, giving the weight, the name of the boat, the skipper and the angler. It is fascinating on the days when you are not fishing to be at the wharves at Pahia or Russell for the weigh-ins between 5.00 and 6.00 pm.

'How exhilarating was the challenge of the mighty trout in the Tongariro River, which flows from the heart of North Island's central volcanic plateau into the six hundred-odd square yards of Taupo Lake, where they feed on Kaura, a fresh-water crawfish. This clear and fast river is claimed, perhaps justly, to be the finest trout river in the world. The rainbow are certainly of great size and renowned for their fighting qual-ities; it once took me twenty minutes to land a seven-pounder.

'The pleasure of fishing here is enhanced by the raw beauty all around, a mystical ambience added by the steam seeping out of volcanic rock, forming low cloud over what in parts seems a lunar landscape. Perhaps it is the volcanic warmth which grows the trout to such size and makes it a place of pilgrimage for trout fishermen the world over. Again, not all the fishermen who come here are expert, and it is possible for the complete novice to come and fish the easy way from boats moored out on the river mouths of Taupo Lake. For instance, my wife had never fished for trout in her life, yet after only an hour's coaching in the casting of a wet fly she was able to enjoy the exquisite thrill of landing three trout, averaging 5 lbs in weight, after a couple of hours' fishing. Now she can't wait to go again! On the same morning, John Reason, the rugby correspondent of the *Sunday Telegraph*, and myself landed six trout weighing 28 lbs, also on the wet fly. It was a grey drizzling heavy morning, so we could only employ a wet fly. The Taupudlians, quite rightly of course, don't regard this as real fishing, but as our time was limited and as it was mid-winter, it was the only method open to us. John and I never fail to 'enliven' rugby tours to New Zealand by visiting the Tongariro to refresh minds jaded by the insular demands of reporting. In 1977 John and I caught eight trout in two hours on the Tongariro, averaging 6 lbs each. None of them took less than ten minutes to land, and it was one of the most exhilarating experiences of my life. Naturally we donated them to the Lions in their hotel in Rotorua, another fine centre for trout fishing.

'Purists, of course, all head upstream for the more demanding art of dry fly fishing but this is quite expensive by New Zealand standards: trout guiding costs approximately 200 New Zealand dollars a day, including all equipment and the licence. The guides, however, are very experienced; they know every ledge and lie, and can almost guarantee a fine catch. Boats can be chartered by the day and for those who can afford it there are helicopters to fly you into the hills for more remote stream fishing.

'The reason for the abundance of trout in New Zealand rivers is largely due to the conservation methods of the New Zealand government. It is illegal to offer trout for sale in shops or to serve it on hotel menus. The only trout you can eat is your own catch. All the hotels are delighted to cook your fish for you, and it really is the end of a perfect day when you enjoy your own fresh, rich trout served with a bottle of good New Zealand dry white wine.

'New Zealand is truly a fishing Valhalla, for in South Island too there are many fast-flowing rivers, full of brown trout, running to the west and east coasts from the southern alps. There is also the fjord land running down from Milford Sound which is alive with spectacular salmon, and the southern lakes between Mount Cook and Queenstown. For me, however, it will always be the Tongariro which claims my affections, for there I have enjoyed the best trout fishing in my lifetime. It has a magic all its own, supported by the most marvellous fishing lodges and hostelries. If you are a trout fisherman and want to fulfil yourself before you die, you must go there – even if it means mortgaging the house for the fare!'

Fishing in New Zealand is free apart from the nominal fee for a licence. No one owns the water even if the land belongs to them. How fortunate they are to have free fishing of higher quality than that for which in Britain people pay £50 a day or more. So prolific are the rainbows that the great numbers of fishermen create no problem in most areas. Indeed were it not for fishing being thus encouraged the size of rainbows might have decreased still further in this area. The excellent spawning grounds in the multitude of rivers flowing into the lake ensure that trout breed in their hundreds of thousands. Now the two hundred and forty square miles of Taupo sustains great shoals of trout but without the wealth of feeding available when they were first stocked, so unless the anglers culled a reasonable proportion there would be too many fish for the water to sustain in good condition.

Both in the North and the South Island there is a great richness of trout waters, but Taupo holds a special place in fishing lore. That is right, for it is a very special place in itself, twelve hundred feet above sea level in the very centre of North Island, with volcanic mountains as a backdrop. There's the forbidding straggle of Tauhara beyond the town of Taupo. In the distance to the east and south lie the ranges of Ahimanawas and Kaimanawas and at the southern end of the lake there are the most dramatic peaks, the snowclad Ruapehu Ngauruhoe with its perfect cone, and the spiky Tongariro. It is all awesome and beautiful with bright Taupo Lake set in the midst.

The main attraction for me, apart from the fish, was that it retains an air of isolation despite the army of anglers around it. I was surprised by the number I encountered as I fished down the Waitahanui River, but though I sometimes had to stop and wait, since it was impossible for two to fish the same small pool, people were never intrusive and soon moved on. As with salmon fishing, it was no harm that they had gone down the water before you: rainbows are always on the move, rarely static in one territorial area like brown trout. Their feeding or attacking instinct also seems to trigger irregularly, so even if a number of flies have already been over its nose a rainbow may suddenly decide to have a dart at another of exactly the same pattern. When we were there in June and July it was winter in New Zealand, though the weather was more settled than in most British summers and the rainbows still in fine condition. My one regret was not seeing it in spring when the great groves of *kowhais* are said to be such a dazzling sight. There was colour enough without them, from the blue-green of rivers splashed with white in their rapids, to the aquamarine of the lake with the mountains mirrored in its surface. Still, I would have liked to see Taupo with its shore ablaze with the gold of the *kowhais* as Kipling did:

> Flung for gift on Taupo's face,
> Sign that spring has come.

Rugby has taken me to two of the most beautiful and most renowned fishing areas in the world. What finer combination of scenery and fish can you imagine than Taupo? Well, how about Vancouver? There's no point arguing the merits of these two: both are matchless but they weren't the only scenes of rugby activity with added interest for fishermen. When I was visiting South Africa in 1980 I was taken for a day's flyfishing on a pleasant trout stream near Newcastle in the Eastern Transvaal. The river itself was slow-moving with clear deep pools. In part the scenery reminded me of Wales with blast furnaces in the background and virgin countryside so close, the Veldt running right up to the industrial town. But the country was wild and a bit mysterious too: what might lurk in the thick undergrowth? I had the creepy feeling that a lion or some other savage beast might be measuring me up as I fished with my back so close to that thick cover but my South African friends laughed at my fears: 'All you need to watch out for is snakes. No lions or alligators here! Africa's a large continent – you're getting your wildlife a bit mixed.' That was comforting, except for the snakes – I was wearing nothing but shorts and gym shoes. There really was a wild and eerie feeling about that river which caught the imagination of my family and friends. When I showed them pictures of it I romanced a little about the unknown animals that might have lurked in the tall grasses. They became so real they actually materialised for some of them in the photographs. 'What a picture!' one of them exclaimed, pointing to a blurred spot in the grass. 'You can even see the lion looking down on you. You had a lucky escape there, Gareth.' Nothing would convince him the image of the lion was only in his mind. Another was sure he saw a crocodile in the water! In reality all the water contained was some plump trout and it wasn't long before I had a nice rainbow of 2½ lb splashing about at the end of my line. Once that was landed I concentrated too hard on catching some more to let the strange surroundings send any more shivers down my spine. It was pleasant water to fish, using size 10 wet flies and casting upstream, but unfortunately I couldn't stay long to enjoy it.

Still, I could never complain at rugby interfering with fishing, since it has introduced me to so many fine rivers and lakes in faraway parts. I didn't try the fishing in Japan and have no regrets about that after hearing John Golding, MP for Newcastle-under-Lyme, recount his experience there. Whenever John's Parliamentary Committee work took him to distant fishy areas his rod went with him. Japan had not seemed the likeliest country in which to find good game fishing, but arriving with a Parliamentary delegation he enquired about the possibilities. His obliging hosts assured him he would have some excellent fishing arranged and expressed their delight at having an eminent angler in the party. In due course he was taken on a long journey into the hills. The drive ended beside a beautiful mountain stream which flowed fast and clear. The banks, however, were lined with Japanese anglers shoulder to shoulder and still fishing, as if in some old print, with long poles and fixed lines such as Izaak Walton himself might have used. Golding saw no fish being caught and was not particularly hopeful when a small area was cleared for his personal use. 'Very Important Guest will catch many fish,' he was assured. It was now seven in the morning and he was handed a pole similar to all the others with line and bare hook attached. The only other tackle was a pile of sticks. Not wishing to let on that the very important guest had no idea how to proceed he waited to see what the nearest angler did. The sticks, it appeared, had to be broken and in the middle was found a suitable grub as bait, to be put on the hook.

After an hour he had caught nothing and there was still no sign of others doing so. 'Very Important Guest, do not worry. You will catch fish at nine o'clock,' they told him. What instinct made Japanese fish feed at precisely nine o'clock, he wondered? By five minutes to the hour he was as yet fishless. At two minutes to, a van drove up and out got the driver to take some large buckets from the back. John had been given an uncomfortable pair of waders to stand in the margins of the stream, and now the bucket carrier advanced and poured a shoal of fish into the water around his legs. Precisely at nine, as forecast, he caught the first of these ravenous, and presumably long starved, fish. Others began catching near him too. After an hour his host told him: 'Very Important Guest, we go home now.' 'I'm just getting into the swing of it,' protested John. 'Please, Very Important Guest, I have counted, and all fish already caught. Nothing more here. We go now.'

A Sunday newspaper once threatened to 'expose' John for fishing on his Parliamentary trips abroad. 'Is it true?' they asked him. 'Certainly,' he replied. 'Surely it's better to be out on the bank with a rod in your hand in your free time than to be propping up the bar? Undaunted, the paper printed its 'revelation'. Far from undermining John, as perhaps the writer had hoped, the 'revelation' that he was a keen fisherman added, by his calculations, some ten per cent support for him in his constituency. They're a sensible lot in Newcastle-under-Lyme, apparently.

It wasn't that type of fishing I regretted missing in Japan. Rugby tours so often inconveniently coincided with the best times for fishing the Towy and the Cothi, and I was worried this one might too. Before I left we'd had a long blank spell with the river low, the fish few and listless; Graham Evans had been joking that as soon as I was out of the way he would clean up. While we waited in the dressing-room for the start of the first international in Osaka our manager, Les Spence, read out a pile of telegrams from wellwishers and eminent rugby personalities. 'This one's for you, Gareth,' he called, 'but it makes no sense. It just reads "Had ten. Bad luck, Gareth. Graham Evans."' It made sense to me all right, and I went out on the field fuming that I had clearly missed the best fishing of the season.

12

Salmon Fishing in the Sea

I've already mentioned Vancouver, another of the world's great fishing centres, which I was fortunate enough to visit as captain of the Welsh team touring Canada. That main northwest coast port is home for great runs of Pacific salmon heading for their remembered rivers, such as the Fraser or the Campbell River on Vancouver Island. Some ten million mature salmon run annually up the Fraser and down it into the ocean come over three hundred million smolts, or parr in the case of Pink and Chum salmon, which go straight to sea without smoltifying. Only about one in thirty survives the hazards and the predators in the deeps to make their one fatal return journey upriver to spawn and die. Because they begin to coarsen, changing shape and colour once they enter fresh water, fishermen hunt them mostly in the sea, where they feed so free and are in prime condition.

There are six species of Pacific salmon. Only the Masu is not found off Vancouver's coast, frequenting instead Asian waters and being successfully bred now in Japanese hatcheries. The Masu is the link between Pacific and Atlantic salmon and from it stemmed the other five, each with very different characteristics. The Chum is also called the 'Dog' because of the large canine teeth it develops at spawning time. It tastes good smoked but otherwise is not highly regarded, indeed Eskimos feed it to their dogs. The adult Chum is a largish salmon averaging 8 to 12 lbs. In salt water it is silvery, with a bluish black and sparse black speckling down its flanks; in fresh water it turns dark, with irregular vertical stripes down the side of its body which may be orange, yellow, purple or dusky red, or any combination of these. Like all Pacific salmon it is an onchorynchus species, with the males developing a pronounced hook nose when back in fresh water.

The Pinks and Sockeyes run small but are very prolific, often moving in great shoals. Sockeyes, in fact, are so uniform in size that commercial fishermen, who had previously relied on Chinese labour to clean and prepare them, were able to instal automatic machinery to do the job. Sockeyes or 'Reds' average 5 to 7 lbs at maturity; in the sea they have brilliant blue to greenish-blue backs and are finely speckled and in rivers they change colour dramatically to end with bright red bodies and green heads. The Pinks or 'Humpbacks' average only 3 to 5 lbs and have a metallic blue back with numerous large indistinct blotches which extend to the tail; the scales are very small, providing a simple distinguishing mark. In fresh water they develop a hump back. The red flesh and high oil content of the Sockeye make them much prized commercially. In a recent year the fishing industry, Canada's third largest, caught and processed 70,604 tons of salmon, 32% of which were Sockeye. Freshly caught Pinks, pale as they look, are nevertheless best for barbecuing. Barbecued salmon, put straight onto the grid or cooked in foil, is one of my happiest memories of Vancouver, the most delicious way of all to prepare this marvellous fish.

For anglers the main prizes are the Coho and Chinook. The Cohos or 'Silvers' or 'Bluebacks' average 6 to 12 lbs but run up to over thirty. They are spectacular fighters, leaping when hooked and continuing to leap as they strip out line at racing speed. Cohos have a bright silvery look and white mouths with white gums; in fresh water they develop a crimson streak along the lateral line which spreads to the rest of the body. The 'kings' of Pacific salmon are the Chinooks, also called 'Springs' and, if over thirty pounds, 'Tyees'. These are the heavyweights which can grow to over a hundred pounds: one of 126 lbs was taken at Petersburg, Alaska, and the world record rod-caught salmon is a Chinook of 92 lbs – that was taken north of Vancouver in the Skeena River, in a tributary of which, the Babine, was also caught the rod record steelhead of 37½ lbs. Chinook can be red- or white-fleshed, but whatever their colour they fight differently from the Coho, using their weight to power down deep and to put persistent strain on the heaviest tackle. These 'kings' have dark backs and large irregular specklings, deeply forked tails, black mouths and gums. Their bodies carry a heavier than usual slime coating, and they give off a pungent acid odour when lifted from the water.

Salmon fishing apart, Vancouver is a city to enjoy, a serene and spacious place as much park as town. There is nothing pretentious in the houses but a pleasant individuality about them with little tract building. Some of the most attractive are in traditional imported styles, such as old colonial, but a more modern and local style was pioneered by architect Ned Pratt, an Olympic oarsman in the 1932 Games who popularised the post-and-beam, flat-roofed, glass-and-cedar-walled house with overhanging eaves. There is much that is innovative in the city architecture, especially the development of derelict industrial sites like Granville Island. This has been converted into a fascinating mix of public markets, art college and theatre, restaurants, marinas, and houseboat 'village'. The houseboats are floating two-storeyed houses with hanging gardens, giving Granville Island a special character; there is even a 'Sea-Village Royal Yacht Club' for the ubiquitous boats moored alongside. Equally imaginative is Gastown, its paved streets embellished with a steam clock and old-fashioned lamp standards, and some of its buildings, such as the Old Spaghetti Factory, attractively combining old and new: you eat inside one of the city's old tramcars re-vamped for diners.

There are many interesting new buildings too, like the Planetarium and the Marine Museum, which houses the historic RCMP ship, *St Roch*. At the start of the Second World War the Canadian Government gave the captain of the *St Roch*, Royal Canadian Mounted Police Sergeant Henry

Larsen, the task of circling the north to re-assert Canadian sovereignty in the Arctic. The *St Roch* took over two years to complete the Northwest Passage from west to east but less than a year to return by the northerly deep-water route. The *St Roch* survived all the hazards of a passage which had claimed so many ships since Frobisher first attempted it in the sixteenth century, and became the first to complete the passage in a single season, the first to travel the northern route, the first to complete the Northwest Passage in both directions, and later the first ship to sail all round the North American Continent when it went through the Panama Canal. The *St Roch* lies in the Marine Museum exactly as she was when eleven 'horse-sailors', with a family of eight Eskimos camped on deck, made their remarkable voyage. Behind them they trailed a 'ship-log', a brass cylinder with metal vanes, its revolutions recording the speed and distance travelled. But it had to be painted black: the shining metal had previously acted like a flasher, attracting sharks to snap it off.

Vancouver is a seaport but without any of the dirt and sleaziness so often associated with them. The trees along the broad streets are a special feature, spreading even into downtown Vancouver, though dwarfed there by the skyscrapers. This is a city which has preserved a fine balance between wood, water and concrete, unique among major cities for having retained so much natural countryside within its limits and surrounds, with a profusion of parks and gardens. In Cypress Park you can see chipmunks and walk down paths imprinted by bobcats and bears. 'Enjoy the bears', says the notice, 'but from a distance.' Across the bay at Point Gray is the campus of British Columbia University, with its Gothic collegiate buildings. It is separated from the heart of Vancouver by its Endowment Lands, over two thousand acres of virgin forest and meadow. Some thirty miles of nature trails wind through it, all with descriptive names like Swordfern, Vine Maple, Huckleberry and Lily of the Valley. The mild wet climate encourages evergreen rain forests in which cedar, hemlock, spruce and other conifers flourish, but Douglas Fir predominates. There are indeed six different types of forest within the Endowment Lands alone, ranging from young alder woods to the peat bog forest of the Camosun Bog. Birds range from black-capped chickadees to golden-crested kinglets to brown-headed cowbirds, the flowers from bleeding hearts to miner's lettuce. The shrubs are varied too, but the main one has a raspberry-like fruit and the highly appropriate name for this area of the salmonberry.

Stanley Park occupies a whole peninsular. One of its present features is the exotic aquarium with everything from performing killer whales to a coelocanth. In the Amazon Section, with its hourly simulated tropical storm, there are sizeable specimens of the Arapaima, the largest of all freshwater fish, growing to thirteen feet or more in length. There's a special section too for game fish and anglers, with all types of British Columbian salmon, trout, char and other species, such as arctic grayling. Its panels explain that the lake 'trout' or northern char are vulnerable to over-fishing, since they grow so slowly; the big ones are twenty years old or more and the largest recorded weighed 102 lbs! Another monstrous fish pictured is a white sturgeon weighing over 800 lbs; it was taken out of the Fraser River in 1962 by Gerald Miller, and about double the weight of a sturgeon recorded as caught in the Towy. The comment here on flyfishing reminds that angling is also the most popular participant sport in North America, as in Britain, and adds: 'Flyfishing is one of the angling techniques which demonstrates artistic and scientific skills which fishermen have developed to enhance their sport.' It does indeed! But salmon inevitably are the main attraction as they have always been. There's a description of the primitive methods employed by the indigenous Indians, whether spearing them or catching them fishing from kayaks using braided hair lines with stone weights attached, and abalone-shell lures given a jerky motion by each stroke of the paddle against which the line was held. For the native coastal peoples of B.C., fishing is a central part of their lives. As the museum puts it: 'The catching of fish is also regarded by them as a spiritual matter, an understanding of the underwater world being a way of knowledge of the spiritual world. A good fisherman prepares himself mentally and physically before a fishing expedition.' With such a belief it's no surprise that the Indians needed no lessons on conservation of the environment. 'The act of throwing rubbish into a river was seen as something unnatural, sure to bring bad luck.' That is a concept being belatedly rediscovered by our modern society.

Of all fish the salmon was the most important to the Indians, so important, indeed, that those of the Northwest Coast were known as the salmon people. The first salmon caught each year was ceremonially prepared and each person in the village received a piece in a celebration intended to ensure the continued arrival of salmon in increasing numbers. It was their belief that the salmon were really people dressed in salmon clothes and that five different tribes of salmon people lived in a village under the sea. Their belief about the birth of mankind is also somewhat different from ours. In the Anthropological Museum at Point Gray, surrounded by impressive totem poles, there's a massive modern sculpture, carved in yellow cedar wood, which expresses the Haida Indians' view of man's beginning. To us it is the legend of the Raven and the Clam. To them it is the story of creation at least as credible as Adam and Eve with the serpent in the Garden of Eden:

'The great flood, which had covered the earth for so long, had at last receded and the sand of Rose Spit lay dry. Raven walked along the sand, eyes and ears alert for any unusual sight or sound to break the monotony. A flash of white caught his eye and there, right at his feet, half buried in the sand, was a gigantic clamshell. He looked more closely and saw the shell was full of little creatures cowering in terror in his enormous shadow. He leaned his great head close and with his smooth trickster's tongue coaxed and cajoled and coerced them to come out and play in his shiny new world. When the little people were inbred with big red rock chitons brown-skinned, black-haired humans finally developed – the Haidas, children of the wild coast. Their descendants would build on its beaches strong, beautiful homes and embellish them with powerful heraldic carvings that told of the legendary beginnings of great families, all the heroes and heroines, the gallant beasts and monsters that shaped their world and their destinies. For many, many generations they grew and flourished, built and created, fought and destroyed, lived according to the changing seasons and the unchanging rituals of their rich and complex lives.'

At least I could share their enjoyment of salmon. From Lions Gate Bridge I watched small boats queue up beneath, trying to catch salmon as they ran past English Bay and into the Capilano River mouth. I heard stories, too, of taking great Springers in the tyee pool at the mouth of Vancouver Island's Campbell River, where they congregate on its sandbar waiting to run upstream. So I eagerly quizzed my opposing captain about fishing opportunities. He disclaimed much interest, but added that inexperienced as he was he had caught three salmon weighing a hundred pounds in total the last time out! The sea-fishing in this area can indeed be so productive that a young girl, Tara Robinson, is experienced enough at age eleven to be writing a monthly fishing column, to have two books on the stocks and another published, entitled *How to Catch Really Big Fish*. By really big fish Tara means salmon averaging over thirty pounds, like the ones she catches. As she puts it, her favourite expressions are: 'Dad, it's just another forty-pounder,' or 'Dad, cut the line. It's too big.' With memories of that woman on the Dee who caught too many salmon too early, I wasn't surprised to read that one of Tara's problems is expressed as: 'Oh no, not *more* fish.' Naturally she recommends catch and release, and amid much expert advice culled from her expert father are such precocious comments as: 'Don't catch the limit. Limit the catch.' A laudable sentiment indeed, but it will be a long time before I'm throwing back double-figure fish unnecessarily!

Of course for most fishermen catching the limit is not that easy, even in British Columbia where daily limits are kept reasonably low – 3 chinook, or 4 salmon of other species, or 8 trout and char. But my appetite had been whetted and I was intrigued to learn of the wide variety of techniques and lures which are used in this sea-fishing. Salmon are taken by trolling, drifting, jigging or mooching, on baits from live herring to 'buzz bombs' to artificial flies. There are of course the usual artificial distinctions between anglers over the imagined ethics, aesthetics or effectiveness of the various methods. Those who play this game put trolling in the lowest grade for 'sporting' content but if you want to 'meat fish' or catch for the pot, or even just think that the object of fishing is to catch fish, then trolling is by far the best bet. You cover larger areas, the speed of the boat should hook the fish for you, and you can use leaders up to 50 lb test, which make the playing easier. The main trolling technique involves the use of weights of up to 2 lbs, preferably slider weights, easy to set at varying distances above the flasher, or dodger, which in turn is a yard or so in front of the lure. Dodgers and flashers are very similar, both metallic or plastic strips some eighteen inches long, the one sweeping from side to side, the other rotating. The lure may also be a plastic or metal spinner, or a hoochie (grey and red strips of material which in the water resemble a small squid), or bucktail flies. But mostly it is an anchovy or a herring, whole or in strip, or plug-cut. Even in trolling there is a 'sporting' distinction: reels have to carry anything up to 500 yards of line, so powerful may be the salmon's surge, and a single action reel, with its greater risk of breaks or knuckle-burn, is regarded by some as a more 'sporting' accessory than, say, a Penn reel with star drag which can be set to control the salmon better and more simply.

Trolling, of course, demands the same kind of skills as harling for salmon in a broad Scottish river: success depends on getting the right lure, in the right place, at the right depth. In a wide expanse of sea and with the different feeding habits of different types of salmon, that can be a complex problem to solve – even the speed requires careful regulation. Two knots is standard. If you increase this to a maximum five knots you'll cover a much wider area but alter the working of your lure, so that it may porpoise up near the surface, unless you get exactly the right equation between length of line and speed of boat. While hooking is automatic to the point that you can put your rod in a holder and read a book until the salmon is on, much depends on the condition of your hooks. Those who keep them needle sharp may improve their catch rate beyond the netting of three out of five takes, which is usually regarded as very satisfactory. Setting the weight, too, can be a matter of fine judgement. Should it be a three-ounce weight to fish nearer the surface, or over a pound to get down deep? How close to the flasher/dodger should it be? The closer it is the less widely the dodger sweeps. When the fish is hooked, the boat should be stopped for the playing; if a heavy tyee seems likely to strip out too much line, then you need to pursue it rapidly rather than attempt any sharp check: let it run is the first rule of playing in the open sea, unless the salmon is headed for kelp beds or any other obvious obstruction.

As in all fishing those who catch the most have a good understanding of the feeding habits of their quarry. They need to know which salmon, such as Pink and Sockeye, may be feeding on tiny red shrimps and are most likely then to be taken with hoochies, the small squid imitations. They need to know when the salmon will be in areas of sandy bottom feeding on sandlance; when close in to shore chasing other small bait fish, like anchovies or minnow herring; when, later, hunting shoals of larger, maturer herring. Especially do they need to know the way salmon feed on herring, preferring to take the crippled fish. When shoals of herring herd together, all of them seek maximum protection in a compact central mass. Into this a salmon will charge, deadly as a torpedo, slapping explosively with its tail, then it will turn to pick up the dazed and injured fish drifting down, as will those salmon following it. When the more aggressive rapacious Coho attack they will fill their mouths overful until dying herring spill out to be taken by other salmon waiting below. So, most lures are hooked up and worked in a way to represent a crippled fish; when trolling strips of herring they need to be trimmed into a shape resembling a pennant or the blade of a hunting knife. Two single hooks are then set in the strip a couple of inches apart in a way which will make the bait wobble and weave like a wounded fish. Whole herring are hooked up with one triple in the nose and another in the back to achieve the same effect.

The methods rated more 'sporting' by some are those which demand greater skill in playing and hooking, with the use of finer tackle with leaders from 10 to 20 lb test and the hand striking home the hook. Jigging qualifies under this head. It involves letting the bait fall free from a still or very slow moving boat then jigging it up and down (being careful not to work the rod so fast the bait is jerked up, or so high that it's impossible to strike hard). The salmon may take on the drop, like a trout taking a nymph, or as the bait is jigged. Often it will only mouth the bait, needing to be struck fast and firm; it may swirl over the bait or slap at it with its tail. So jigging is sometimes classed as 'unsporting' since a number of salmon get themselves foul-hooked that way. Jigging is best suited to fishing off piers or anchored boats or rafts. Drift fishing similarly involves finer tackle and no use of a motor, best practised when there are shoals of small bait fish close to shore. Sometimes salmon will follow the bait up towards the boat – that's the most exciting moment of all if the water is clear enough to see them. As with a rainbow trout following a fly, you may trigger it into attacking by slowing or stopping the retrieve.

The most popular of the 'sporting' techniques is mooching. As its name implies, it's a slow, reflective form of fishing though its more expert exponents certainly don't 'wander aimlessly'. Experienced locals will know exactly where and at what depth to mooch. One of them defined the term for me as using light tackle for still or slow fishing, with no weights, dodgers or flashers. At its 'purest', mooching is a form of still fishing involving a longish rod with a pliant and sensitive tip, a simple single action reel without gears or bales, and a light line of 10 to 15 lb test, with either herring strip or live herring for bait. The moocher should be personally involved in setting the hook and must play the fish without encumbrance of weights. However, the term does embrace a wide range of options including 'power mooching', strip casting, and even plug-cut trolling. One of the most effective forms of mooching is the old Indian method of rowing in short bursts and in between letting the bait spiral down in an arc as might a crippled herring. Mooching appealed to me most as a concept, but the very experienced fishermen who took me out used a form that the purists don't recognise as mooching. This was mooching in deep water using a down-rigger, a fine steel wire of 100 lb plus test, paid out from a drum on the side of the boat with a seven- or eight-pound weight attached. This is clipped to your line with a gadget resembling a clothes peg, so that the down-rigger can plummet it down a hundred feet or more.

The 'take' was an unusual sensation. The small, powerful rod was bowed from the heavy weight but when the salmon struck there was no solid pull or further arch of the rod tip: instead it sprang straight and the line went slack as though I'd lost the fish. The pull of the salmon released my line from the clip, leaving feet of slack before the surge of the fish took it up and had the rod jerking wildly. I caught none of the thirty-pounders but how well the smaller salmon fought on the light tackle! That at least was a real excitement for me though the techniques did not attract me as much as river fishing. But then I was simply the rod-holder and fish-player: the real skills were with those who set up my lures and took me to fishy places – the red Bell Buoy off Point Gray, or over to Horseshoe Bay, or out to Vancouver Island. My boat was one of a number equipped with every device to locate and catch salmon, including echo-sounders. Like the salmon they hunted, the expert fishermen seemed to shoal together, finding the best place and gathering the boats there. How different from the lonely concentration of the angler on a river! This was in part a friendly social meeting of old friends, with the boats floating gin-palaces, and much banter between the crews. It is not only salmon which you hook. Lingcod, or the shark-like dogfish, may as easily seize the bait. Locals could instantly spot the difference: when a salmon is hooked it moves off fast, slanting the line away at a speed no cod or dogfish can match. So when I imagined myself into my first salmon I was rapidly disillusioned by the surrounding boats setting up a chorus of barking. And a dogfish it was – though the salmon followed soon after.

Apart from natural baits there are some specialist artificial ones. The Stingsilda was originally a Norwegian cod bait. Some samples were advertised in a Vancouver shop with an offer of money back if no cod were caught on them. Some Chinese cod fishermen bought the bait and returned later angrily demanding their money back as all it appeared to catch was a lot of salmon! It's sold well since. So has the Deadly Dick, a heavyweight spin fishing lure in a variety of weights from half to two ounces, and a variety of recommended colours for fishing at different depths. Most effective of all is the 'Buzz Bomb', invented by Rex Field, to simulate in motion an injured herring and also to give out sonic vibrations to attract fish out of sight. Sound can play a part in attracting salmon and even in trolling it is desirable that the line vibrates or 'sings'. Conversely, smell can put fish off their food, just as it may discourage humans. So cleanliness of hands and tackle is a fetish with some of the best fishermen.

The best times for taking salmon are the two hours after dawn or the last two before dusk, but they may come on to feed any time of day. You can take them at night too, if you fish from or round lighted piers or wharves: the light attracts small bait fish, and their shoals soon attract salmon. In winter salmon may be feeding close to the surface at dawn, but in full daylight will be sixty to a hundred feet down; most salmon, in fact, are caught deep down. However, at times there were many to be seen jumping or cruising purposefully along on the surface and so they could often be taken by trailing buck-tailed flies, hoochies, flashtails, or other hairy or flutter-tail lures close to the top. Roger Wiewel, an executive of MacMillan Bloedel, recently found an unusual way of doing this. He is an expert wind-surfer and what he did standing up was to catch a

Coho by using a flyrod and trailing a bucktail behind on a short line while surfing. The derision of the conventional boat fishermen changed rapidly when he hooked his fish. Lowering the sail he played it standing on the board and netted it in the sail when it was played out. Despatching it was a problem until a helpful boat edged in, and lent him the traditional wooden billy club.

A feature of salmon fishing in British Columbia is the many competitions ranging from the Daiwa World Salmon Championship, fished over many weeks from May to September, to hidden weight competitions in which the winner is the one with a salmon closest to the species and weight known in advance only to the judges. Prizes can be very large but none as large as that offered in a competition off Seattle, just across the border. Five tagged salmon were released into the sea and a million dollar prize was offered for any caught in the competition. Two were taken, so a couple of lucky anglers became dollar half-millionaires.

The most popular competitions are the many local salmon derbys which may attract two thousand or more boats, with an average of three or more rods in each. The local Vancouver paper, *The Sun*, has run the Sun Free Salmon Derby annually for almost half a century. In 1983 the winner, Paul Sidsworth, acquired a seventeen-foot Hourston glasscraft boat, a ninety horse-power outboard motor, a loader-trailer, plus life-vests and a quantity of tackle. All the first three won boats and motors, and apart from handsome prizes for the top ten there were other special prizes. The prizes related solely to the heaviest fish caught. Sidsworth's was over 28 lbs and came complete with angler's tale. It was hooked on an old rod in dilapidated condition and took seventy minutes to land; at one stage it tangled round another competitor's anchor chain, which he sportingly cut off to help free the line. When Sidsworth netted it his small net broke, and another competitor came alongside to lend him one of the massive nets in common use. The derby had started at dawn with the weigh-in at Horseshoe Bay at 2.30 p.m.; the salmon was hooked late in the contest and after all these adventures Sidsworth made it back with only thirty seconds to spare. Of the fish which won him so much he commented scornfully that it was 'only a little gaffer in derby terms'. Seeing it took him so long to land he was perhaps fortunate it wasn't the seventy-one pounder caught in the Rivers Inlet off Vancouver Island a month later by a mooching angler, Bob Tennant.

In Vancouver a seven-pound licence brings you the province-wide freedom of lakes and rivers generously supplied with game fish. Unfortunatley I had no chance to fish for steelhead in the rivers, that sea-going rainbow which is the fiercest fighter of them all. Nor was there an opportunity for distant expeditions to fishing camps in Kamloops or Okanagan, where trout run large and numerous. It was a Kamloops rainbow which set the world rod caught record at 48 lbs. Kamloops rainbows had flourished in lowland lakes but barriers in the streams had prevented them reaching many of the mountain waters. Then, in 1908, the Canadian Fish Cultural Service stocked the lakes. By the 1930s, when the record was set, these stocked trout had grown to vast size but, as at Taupo Lake, once they proliferated and the feed declined so did the average weight, and that record is probably unassailable now.

In the remoter areas of British Columbia there are countless acres of little fished water well stocked with rainbows, with brown trout, or with the cut-throat, which has that distinctive slash of red under the jaw; or with the three main species of char – the northern lake 'trout', the eastern brook 'trout', or the Dolly Varden, the most colourful of them all with its speckling of pale yellow or orange to red spots. In many lakes you may find the Kokanees, the land-locked salmon. But you don't have to fly off to the interior to catch some of these in wild surroundings. From North Vancouver the British Columbia Railway takes you in a couple of hours into the high mountains where the fishing is good in spring and fall and the skiing good in winter. There are breathtaking views from the train along Howe Sound to Britannia Beach, with its Mining Museum offering to let you pan for gold, and on past Squamish up to Whistler. Against a backdrop of the Blackcomb Mountain, with its World Cup ski slopes, you can fish in the emerald green waters of glacial lakes or you can spin or flyfish in mountain rivers like the Cheakamus, with its foaming white runs and fast glides, now clear, now cloudy with that distinctive colour of snowfed streams. In the lower reaches of the Cheakamus you can take salmon and steelhead outside its close seasons of 1st April to end of June and 16th August to end of September. Above the cataracts of the canyon in its middle reaches you can catch a profusion of rainbows and some Dolly Varden, with dry fly very effective in the stretch below the Daisy Lake Dam. The rainbows are not large and there's nothing remarkable about them except that you may catch and release the occasional one bright red all over after spawning. But there is a fascination about fishing the Cheakamus which is enhanced by its majestic setting amid the quiet grandeur of the snowcapped peaks and pine-clad slopes. There's a feeling of freedom and exhilaration there reflected in place names like the Singing Pass. It is a small stream flowing between Alta and Green Lakes whose name best expresses the attraction of the fishing: the River of Golden Dreams.

For the game fisherman British Columbia is indeed a dreamland, justifying the obligatory description on car number plates of Beautiful British Columbia. But to enjoy it to the full you still have to be a competent angler. As the local fishing guide puts it: 'Contrary to popular belief luck has little or nothing to do with an angler's ability *consistently* to catch fish. As in any sport you must be astute, alert, and willing to work in order to achieve some degree of proficiency.' The official statistics, like all official statistics, need to be treated with considerable scepticism, but they do show trends. They record that in 1960 in British Columbia 175,203 licensed anglers caught eight million game fish averaging 3.8 per rod day. In 1980 475,325 caught the same number, averaging only 1.5 per rod day. Even in paradise you can blank out if you don't have the ability and experience.

13

Reflections on the Waters

Nothing in my life has given me more pleasure over a longer period than my fishing. It has been a passionate interest from my early childhood, ensuring countless hours of happiness, so a natural concern of mine is that my own children and the generations to come should all have proper opportunity to enjoy this marvellous sport. There is a special affinity between man, the rivers of his environment and their fish. Andrew Lang wrote powerfully of that attraction: 'The passion, or instinct, being in all senses blind, must no doubt be hereditary. But I would as soon lay down a love of books as a love of fishing. Success with pen or rod may be beyond one, but there is the pleasure of pursuit, the rapture of endeavour, the delight of an impossible chase, the joys of nature – sky, trees, brooks, and birds. Happiness in these things is the legacy to us of the barbarian. Man in the future will enjoy bricks, asphalte, fog, machinery, "society". We are fortunate who inherit the older, not "the new spirit". We follow our father, Izaak, by streams less clear, indeed, and in meadows less fragrant, than his. Still they are meadows and streams not wholly dispeopled yet of trout.'

That was perceptive writing for the turn of the century and it still strikes a chord today. We are indeed fortunate who inherit the same primeval love of rivers and fish which persists worldwide, as in those Indians on Canada's west coast. There is an almost mystic attraction about the sport and one which embraces a respect, reverence even, for the quarry. For man is also a conservator, helping fish to survive in an environment made more hostile by an industrial outlook which has often been cavalier in regard to pollution. When Hugh Falkus was visiting the Llandyssul Angling Association waters he commented to Artie Jones that Wales had as fine a resource of salmon and sea-trout rivers as had Scotland, but that in the past much of it had been wantonly squandered rather than sensibly developed. There is certainly no harking back to the 'good old days' in Wales, for the worst of the damage is nearly a century old. Indeed, the situation was far worse then with many rivers cleared of fish by the pollution from mines and industrial plant. As a frustrated Fishery Inspector, Mr Ffennell, wrote in 1866 about the existing attitudes: 'A miner will go to any lengths and any distance for the water required for his machinery or to clean his ore. He will even throw wooden aqueducts across obstructive valleys. But ask the same man to allow the fish to live in the rivers below, the poultry to pick up the sand without being killed, the cattle to drink the water or eat the herbage without fear of "bellan" and you will find the expense of digging the few catch pits or laying a few fathoms of wooden open pipe will, according to him, absorb the whole profits of his enterprise!' Augustus Grimble's famous book pictured this in stark detail as he wrote of the rivers in the south of Wales: 'the poison refuse of copper, lead, tin, iron, and coal works' was making it nearly certain that 'salmonidae will never again frequent these streams'. He added: 'The rivers falling into the north shores of the Bristol Channel and the Bays of Swansea and Camarthen are for the most part worthless as far as salmon angling is concerned.' In the Mawddach River gold was the source of all evil and the mine concerned earned this stern rebuke from Grimble: 'The Gwynfynydd Gold Mine is the source of obnoxious and wanton pollution. Surely, if the mine is worthy of its auriferous title it should be able to afford the outlay of a little of its gold in making settling tanks.'

Of the Taff, Rumney and Ely he wrote that in 1901 they were as fishless as the Ebbw, with only one rod licence issued that year between them all! Happily in Wales, as in England, great efforts have been made in recent years to control pollution and to clean up affected rivers. In boyhood I fished the Tawe, which once had a reputation for excellent runs of sea-trout. In time it became so polluted by waste from heavy industry that it was just another worthless fishing river. But the companies and the authorities have worked so effectively on the problem that the Tawe is now relatively clean again and with reasonable runs of sea-trout, just one example of how quickly a fine river can become barren of migratory fish and how hard it is to restore. But at least the ordinary forms of pollution are now better understood and the more determined efforts at control are having an effect. But with that problem being vigorously tackled there is a new, more elusive menace, and one which in the long term may perhaps be even more dangerous. Acid deposition, or acid rain, is a phenomenon whose effects as yet are imperfectly understood, either in the atmosphere or in the environment. So far Britain has not suffered the devastation of parts of Scandinavia or Germany or North America but many lakes and rivers in Scotland have already been affected. In Wales the increasing acidification of some of the waters, particularly in Dyfed and Gwynedd, has caused concern over the last seven years or more. The Welsh Water Authority has recognised and publicised the problem and has taken the first steps to counter this insidious threat. In 1983 a comprehensive monitoring programme was initiated and over the following three years some £100,000 is being devoted to researching the subject, with close co-operation with scientists in Scotland and Scandinavia. But the problem really is an international one, with the recipients of the acid deposit rarely being its originators. There is no quality of mercy for the fish as the acid rains down on those beneath, though some Scottish trout have already adapted to surviving a certain degree of acidification.

Those countries which are suffering worst are often least able to control the problem which probably has its origins elsewhere. The scale of the threat must be appreciated internationally and dealt with internationally, even if it does involve great expense and inconvenience for governments or the polluting industries. The resources to deal with it are as vast as the problem, however, and the threat is not just to rivers and fish but to many aspects of our environment, as must be plain enough by now. It is good to see action being taken in Wales and we must hope that elsewhere that earlier, penny-pinching attitude which allowed so much unnecessary pollution from mines and other sources in the past will not recur. So far there has been no dramatic example in Wales of acidification wiping out fish and other life in lakes or river systems, as has happened in Sweden, but the warning signs are there. For example, Llyn Berwyn is now fishless, and salmon and sea-trout are unable to survive in the headwaters of the Towy. The need for preventive action clear enough.

Another main threat to salmon – the vast quantities netted at sea – is also an international one. The swiftly increasing catches round the Faroes, the doubts about Greenland's continuing acceptance of quotas, the alleged drastic effect of monofilament nets – all these have created a danger to the existence of Atlantic salmon which can only be dealt with by governments with assistance from specialist bodies like the Atlantic Salmon Trust. The 'harvesting' countries which net the fish as they swim by their coasts, and the 'ranching' countries in whose rivers the salmon are produced, do have conflicting interests, but they surely have a common one, too, in their long-term need to preserve adequate stocks; and that should aid co-operation and moderation.

Moderation, however, is notably absent from the illegal netting and gang poaching activities estimated to take in some rivers and tidal waters as many migratory fish as the licensed netsmen. There may be, to some, something romantic about the small poacher but there can be nothing acceptable in these large-scale depredations. 'The gentle art of poaching', it is sometimes called, but there is nothing gentle in gang violence or in the use of Cymag, or cyanide. This kills in brutal fashion not only the salmon and sea-trout but the trout, the parr and everything else living in the affected pool. The monofil net is almost as deadly, so invisible in the water that not even the salmon's highly developed sense of preservation warns it away, and so light that lengths over a thousand yards can be easily transported and stowed in a boat. As Douglas Sutherland wrote in *The Salmon Book*: 'Some of the poachers admit that this large-scale poaching, coupled with the deep-sea netting in the Atlantic, will inevitably result in there eventually being no salmon. Their attitude is that this is regrettable, but not a compelling reason for them to at least attempt to limit their depredations.' So, it is essential that other ways are found of limiting them. Sutherland's is no fanciful comment. The dangers of failing to control mass poaching were made clear enough even a century ago, when the Teifi had minimal runs of migratory fish because of the proliferation of illegal nets and the universality of poaching. According to Augustus Grimble, though the close season for nets started as late as 3rd November, even this was not observed. In addition 'spears and lights were ceaselessly plied on the spawning beds, while fry was openly captured and openly sold throughout the district.'

In relation to its size more nets were at work on the Teifi than any other river in Britain. With such massive illegal poaching as well, salmon stocks were brought so low that in 1868 'scarcely a salmon was captured by rod'. Indeed so little was there for the angler to catch that only twenty-three bothered to fish the Teifi that season. Shortly after, when the Teifi Conservators attempted to improve the salmon stocks by blowing up some of the rocks at Cenarth, a major obstacle to migratory fish, they fell foul of the organised poachers. The obstacle had made poaching there easy and when the workmen arrived they were 'stoned off the river and when they were routed their tools, barrows, and planks were broken in pieces and thrown into the water.'

How can the modern menace be controlled, since self-restraint is an unlikely solution? The Ministry of Agriculture, Fisheries and Food issued in July 1981 a Consultation Paper reviewing inland and coastal fisheries in England and Wales.

Among its many suggestions were that the Sea Fisheries Committees and Water Authorities should work more closely together. Included were a couple of important proposals on detail. The first was that in the designated Sea Fishery Committee Areas the use of nets considered capable of taking salmon should be proscribed unless specifically licensed for that purpose. The second was one which should have a much more widespread effect and very likely prove the best way of limiting large-scale illegal netting and poaching: control of the sale of salmon after landing would hit at 'commercial' gangs. Licensing of all those dealing in salmon has been thought impractical because of problems and expense of administering and overseeing some three thousand retail outlets; as an alternative a Private Member's Bill in 1977 sought to make it illegal to possess or sell salmon unless it could be proved that they were legally caught, but that failed because it breached the laws of natural justice – that a man is innocent unless proved guilty. But much thought has been given to the matter since then and as the Consultation Paper indicated: 'To overcome this difficulty, possibilities have been explored for providing proof that salmon had been caught legally; for example, by the tagging of salmon destined for sale at special landing centres which would not interfere with existing wholesale and retail channels.' The Water Industry's proposals, published by the former National Water Council (now the Water Authorities Association), go much further than this, with all licensed net and rod fishermen having to use authorised tags on their salmon as soon as landed, and the possession or sale of any untagged salmon then being illegal.

There was some expectation that the Green Consultation Paper would be followed by a White Paper and then by legislation. Two and a half years later little has changed but urgent consideration is now being given to developing some form of tagging control, and the National Water Council's pressure for this has had strong backing from individuals in both Houses of Parliament. The extent of the menace of illegal netting has at least been realised and the means are there to combat it with reasonable chance of success. But action is needed too before long in order to preserve our migratory fish stocks from this additional threat.

The level of legal netting in rivers and river mouths has been a major problem on occasions in the past, when it was less well controlled than now. On the Teifi in 1881, for instance, the *licensed* nets took a declared total of 87,360 lbs of salmon against a rod catch of less than 300 lbs! Matters deteriorated further when the netsmen developed the 'shot fawr' or great net, by joining many nets together and covering the whole river mouth so that hardly any fish got through. Apart from complaints by anglers, such was the outcry from coracle owners, whose rights go back much further than the netsmen's, and from hoteliers dependent on anglers' custom, that the 'shot fawr' did not survive long.

It has always been a difficult matter to balance the rights and needs of netsmen with those of riparian owners and fishermen, and this was the subject of close examination in 1983 in the Report of an Inquiry into objections against an order and bye-laws made by the Welsh Water Authority. The Inspector responsible for the report was A. N. Marshall, the Assessor, B. Stott, Inspector of Salmon and Freshwater Fisheries, MAFF. The report had this to say of the facts of the present situation: 'Over the last hundred years or so in Wales there has been a dramatic change in the way migratory fisheries have been exploited. In 1868 there were 509 nets of various kinds in use and only 481 rod and line anglers. In 1980 the number of nets had been reduced to 152, while the number of licensed rod and line anglers had increased enormously to 22,191. The total number of individuals employed in net fishing totalled some 700 in 1979; 144 of these had been licensees, while the others were endorsees casually employed by the licensee. Catch returns in 1980 showed that netsmen had caught 6,203 salmon and 13,319 sea trout, while those with rod licences had caught a total of 5,477 salmon and 22,446 sea trout. The licence revenue from netsmen fell far below the cost to the Welsh Water Authority of providing the present level of services to them. Before 1980/81 expenditure allocated to nets was calculated at £108,000 while the income was projected at only £10,000. The deficit of £98,000 was a charge to the environmental services element of the water rate paid by the public.'

The report then indicated that the Authority had attempted to evaluate the overall monetary worth of the commercial net fisheries compared to the rod fisheries. The net fisheries' annual value was estimated at £246,000 in 1981 against the rod fisheries' value of £8,000,000. From these facts the Inspector concluded that a change of emphasis was overdue, particularly taking into account the attitude of anglers: 'Their first aim was the protection of the stock in their rivers; their secondary aim was, once the stock was protected, to claim a greater share of the catch than they had at present. Anglers made a vastly greater total contribution to the Water Authority's licence revenue than did the netsmen, and received comparatively little in return. In addition to their licence fees, anglers have to pay heavily for the privilege of fishing in rentals, rates and so on. Netsmen on the other hand, have no rates or rents or sporting rights to pay.'

The Inspector proposed therefore that urgent consideration should be given to amending the law so that in future full account can be taken of the purpose for which stock is to be conserved. He added: 'In my view the time has come when the salmon and sea-trout fisheries should be managed primarily for the benefit of the licenced rod and line anglers, net fishing being limited to such an extent as is compatible with the maintenance of stock at optimum level in the upper reaches of the river.'

Naturally that view appeals to anglers but, like the Inspector, one must recognise that due regard has to be paid 'to the traditions of net fishing – which, in the case of coracle fishing, stretches back thousands rather than hundreds of years – and the contribution which netting of salmonids makes to the income of those engaged in it'. This is no simple problem but being sympathetic to netsmen's interests doesn't prevent anglers from taking heart from the Inspector's conclusions: 'It would be quite wrong to ignore the tremendous changes which have taken place since the last century. Rod and line angling is now a recreational outlet of great importance for many thousands of people from all walks of life. I was deeply impressed during the inquiry by the commitment of the anglers to their cause, expressed not only in the money and time devoted to the inquiry, but also in the way that witnesses for the Welsh Salmon & Trout Angling Association gave their evidence. Fishing for salmon and sea-trout, with some chance of reasonable catches, is a matter of burning concern to a great many people.'

But whatever the proper balance between licenced rod and licenced net fishing, that is only a minor part of the problem. For both parties the more pressing concern is the attack on illegal fishing. As the Inspector commented: 'There was much evidence during the inquiry as to the extent of illegal fishing on both tidal and non-tidal water. All parties expressed great concern at this. In my view that is right. Where stocks are endangered to the extent that it becomes essential to reduce the level of exploitation, the first priority should in equity be to concentrate on the elimination of illegal exploitation. I accept that the Water Authority are making great efforts in this direction, but I fully appreciate the difficulties in enforcing the law over a very wide area against determined and often well-organised poachers. The difficulty is particularly apparent in those areas where salmonids are taken by sea fishermen who, although not licensed to catch salmon or sea-trout, fish perfectly legitimately for other species. This problem is particularly serious near the mouths of the Dee and Usk. The importance of controlling and, so far as possible eliminating, illegal fishing for salmon and sea-trout cannot be over-emphasised. While I fully share the Water Authority's reservations as to the accuracy of the catch returns at their disposal, there is at least some information, however flawed, as to the quantities of fish caught by licensed fishermen; there is no such indication of the illegal take. I therefore recommend that the

Authority's efforts be directed towards the eradication of illegal fishing be maintained, and where possible, intensified, and that further urgent consideration be given to the possibility of legislative action to make the Authority's task easier.'

Angling is such an individual and carefree sport that the millions who enjoy it are loath to combine to press their cause but that recommendation deserves to have wide support from all fishing interests. The lovely rivers of Wales and their stock of game fish have great importance as a social amenity, as a source of pleasure, as a tourist attraction, and as a source of work and wealth for many. Those of us who have had such enjoyment from them, and from our fishing, can only hope that the measures which are in our power to take are taken in time to preserve this national resource. Fishing has given me the happiest of memories. But it is more important that the prospects should remain good for the 'gleaming, untravelled future' Andrew Lang spoke of, in which I and my children and the company of anglers may continue to enjoy the contentment and happiness of fishing in rivers not dispeopled of game fish.